In the Books

Donald Colson

Copyright © 2023 by Donald Colson

All rights reserved.

No portion of this book may be reproduced in any form without written permission from the publisher or author, except as permitted by U.S. copyright law.

Contents

01. First Day	1
02. Memories	15
03. Competition	25
04. It Pours	35
05. Baby Steps	48
06. Pressure	57
07. Mixed Feelings	68
08. Paintings	77
09. Their Place	84
10. Suck It Up (Take One)	96
11. Hardwork	105
12. Loosen Up	113
13. Suck It Up (Take Two)	122

14. Future	135
15. Connection	143
16. Hope	155
17. Feelings	166
18. His Heart	175
19. Get In, Loser	186
20. Heartfelt	200
21. Be My Guest	210
22. Drama	224
23. Changes	240
24. Sorting It Out	249
25. New Truths	260
26. Revealed	270
27. New Faces	285
28. Accomplishments	296
29. Sweet Like Candy	307
30. Coming Out	316
31. Arrangements	327
32. Their Story	340

01. First Day

RYLIE

WE ALL HAVE various versions of ourselves. The two I have most are the one I show to everyone else, hiding certain feelings that we don't want others to notice, and the one I show to myself.

There are just evolving feelings that no one would understand. Grief, anxiety, and heartbreak all wrapped into one. It's always challenging to talk about these emotions to others, especially since they're from the past.

But right now, I don't have the energy or time to talk about it with anyone. Today, I will be starting my senior year in high school. I've been dreading this day since . . . forever. Especially since I'll have to be around loads of people and answer questions from teachers. Most of the other students are excited for today and would practically chat their hearts out nonstop with others.

Don't get me wrong. A lot of people think that I'm a shy person who hates being social and never says a peep. In reality, I'm socially awkward and an outsider. I'd rather be hidden in the dim shadows of trees at night than to be in the spotlight of anything.

I wasn't always like this. When I was a young child, I was quite chatty, as a lot of people I knew would say. Whether it would be at dinnertime or at school, I always had something to say. People wonder how I had gone from being a motormouth to an inaudible mouse. In short words, it's complicated.

Let's just say that certain events from my past caused me to become this silent.

"Rylie, sweetie, have a great day at school. Love you," Mom chimed after taking a sip of her tea. "And don't forget to keep your head up at all times!"

"Fine, I won't. I'll see you later," I mumbled, swinging my dense backpack over my shoulder.

I sighed heavily as I exited the car, closing the door shut behind me. Crowds of students overfilled the front area of the school, chatting as loud as they could. I bit my lip as my knees trembled. My instincts told me to go back inside the car, lie to Mom that I feel "sick", and go back home to skip the school day.

There's a heavy chance that she would make me go to school anyway, especially since I looked fine earlier this morning. But it's worth a try, right?

Wrong.

When I peered back at where Mom's car was parked when she dropped me off, she was already gone. Now, I will have to hope that I will survive this school day in one piece. It will be a challenge.

The immense school building stood firmly against the sky as the sun continued to rise, multiple hues fading into one. The crisp, early September air blew the country flag that stood tall on a pole that stood next to the school. Crews High School is one of the most popular schools in my city, which means that there are a lot of students. Believe me, it isn't good for my socially awkward self.

But now, I will have to try to set that aside. I trudged my way through the students who blocked the path to the entrance, avoiding eye contact with every single one of them. They're probably not looking at me, since most of them are catching up with their friends or whatever, but still.

When I got inside the school, the first thing I saw was a familiar-looking girl with her back glued to the wall.

She had her long, wavy raven hair that hung over her shoulders. She wore a plain beige turtleneck shirt, a tan plaid skirt that reached to above her knees, and white sneakers to match. I could recognize a look like that anywhere. It was my best and only friend, Nora Reyes.

Instead of her being quiet like me, she's loud and outgoing. She sometimes encourages me to branch out and step outside of my comfort zone a bit, but of course, I do the opposite whenever she says that. I never know where to start when it comes to stepping outside of my comfort zone.

It's just . . . difficult.

Other than that, she has a fantastic fashion sense. Nora wears a wide variety of colorful skirts, jeans, leggings, turtlenecks, sweaters, crop tops, and everything else you could possibly think of when it comes to clothing. Sometimes, I feel like I want to raid her closet and snag anything that would fit my style (since I mostly wear hoodies and sweaters) and borrow them.

"Nora, hey!" I exclaimed with a wave.

"Ry, you're finally here. I've been waiting for you for like, forever," Nora chimed, resting her arm around my shoulder.

"Yeah . . . I hope this day goes by quickly. I don't want to be here," I grimaced, glimpsing at the people who bolted through the doors.

"It'll go by quicker than you think. It's just the first day," she assured me.

I hope that Nora is right, because if not, I won't have a great day. School is one of my most dreaded places. There are many places I'd rather be, like the comfort of my bedroom where no one is watching, or the public library. Rows upon rows of books stood on wooden bookshelves, waiting to be taken and read.

The library is a quiet place, so much to the point where you could hear a clock ticking if you were near it. There's not a lot of people, making it a perfect place for me.

"So . . . let's go see what classes we have together and pick up our schedules!" Nora suggested, motioning me towards a nearby stairway that was packed with people.

I nodded with a gulp and followed her on the staircase. So far, it's a mystery of how many classes I have with Nora. I hope that I'll have most of them with her. If I don't, then I'll end up alone in classes.

Just imagine when we do group work or work with a partner. My socially awkward self wouldn't know what to do. Working with someone in class that isn't Nora is a nightmare, petrifying enough to make my teeth chatter and my bones shiver.

All I know about the two of us having a class together is that we're certain to have art, an elective both of us signed up for this year. Originally, I didn't want to have art this year. The reason why I have it is because my mother kept pestering me about how I should try something new, step out of my comfort zone, and branch out.

She isn't wrong, but like I said earlier, I don't know how to step out of my comfort zone. Heck, I don't even know where to start. I guess trying something new, like me taking an art class is going to be a start.

I have mixed feelings about it, but on the bright side, I'm sure that art class doesn't require being social with people.

Right?

After six long hours of going from class to class, it was finally time for art. Nora and I walked together from our last class, which we had together. It turned out that we had five classes together, which is good enough for me.

All of the art classes were located on the west side on the ground level of our school, so we had to walk quite a distance to arrive. The door of our art class was wide open. The first thing I saw were the vivid decorations, such as paper flowers and cutouts that stuck to the wall. Paper honeycombs of all sizes hung from the ceiling from left to right.

The classroom was packed with students who whispered to each other inaudibly. It was so packed to the point where there were hardly any empty seats left in sight.

I looked towards the back of the classroom to see if there were any available seats. Unluckily, all the seats were filled. In fact, the only empty seats were in the front.

Great.

I feel more comfortable sitting in the back of a classroom. No one will bother to look at me or anything. But now, I have to sit in the front. Nora motioned me to a table that had three people sitting on it. There were two boys that sat next to each other, while the other sat across one of them.

That left two available chairs to sit on, right across each other. I avoided eye contact from anyone who could be staring at me and sat next to one boy, while Nora sat next to another.

Our teacher, Ms. Edwards, a young woman who looked like she was in her late twenties, stood in front of the class with a broad smile spread across her face. She cleared her throat and adjusted one of the sleeves of her tie-dyed T-shirt.

"Hello, everyone. Welcome to art class," she proclaimed as she headed towards the door to close it. "I'm Ms. Edwards, and I will be your art teacher for this year."

Her smile continued to broaden as she glimpsed at every part of the classroom. She strutted to her desk and projected a presentation that she would review with us.

She took a few minutes to introduce herself to us by saying basic things about herself, such as her passion for art. That explained the decorations that were hung all around the room.

After that, she explained how her class is about creativity, not perfection. She also went over some information about the materials we would use in class.

Typical stuff.

"For the remainder of this class period, you all will do a pre-test," Ms. Edwards smiled, flipping her sleek, strawberry blonde hair to her shoulder.

A chorus of groans and people sucking their teeth erupted. Taking a test can be a handful. But on the first day of school when everyone's in the process of turning their brains back on for the school year? That's just a whole different thing.

"Don't worry, people. It won't be a written or standardized test. It will be something . . . fun," Ms. Edwards added, clasping her hands together. "You all will create a drawing of anything you'd like. Sketch everything out first and then start drawing. Do as much as you can before class is over."

"Will this be graded?" A student from the back of the classroom questioned.

"No, but I expect everyone to try their best," the teacher replied. "Remember, this isn't about perfection. This is about creativity!"

Ms. Edwards picked up a stack of papers from her desk and strutted towards our table. She handed the papers to the boy who sat next to me.

"Can you please pass these out for me, Elias?" She queried.

"Yeah, I will, Ms. Edwards," Elias stood up from his stool.

He handed a paper out to me first, then everyone else that sat at our table. He circled around the classroom and gave a paper to each student, getting some type of thank you from each of them. When he finished passing the papers out, he strutted to his seat and sat down.

I placed my bulky backpack on my lap to search for a pencil. I rummaged through notebooks, a planner, folders, loose sheet protectors, and pens, still not finding a pencil. Before school started today, I was in a rush to put all my supplies in my backpack since I didn't pack them beforehand, which is why it's messy.

I should find the time to organize everything.

Luckily, I found a mechanical pencil laying at the bottom of my backpack, on top of a spiral notebook I used today for History. I pulled it from there and placed my backpack on the floor.

I grimaced and raised an eyebrow as I glimpsed at my paper. I have no clue on what to draw. Heck, I'm not even good at drawing. I can hardly manage to draw a straight line, even if it's a teeny-weeny line.

Okay, fine; maybe I can draw a teeny-weeny line—like a minus sign straight. But anything that's an inch or two longer than that, nope.

"So, Ry, what are you going to draw for your picture? I'm going to draw myself from when I was in a cool resort in the Philippines, just like I did this summer," Nora exclaimed, grabbing the attention of everyone at our table.

"I don't know what to draw . . ." I murmured, stroking my pencil across my paper. "I think I'll draw me and my pet cat, Cookie."

"That sounds cute," she beamed with a grin.

Cookie is my other best friend. I've been her owner for about a year now. Usually, when I come home from somewhere, she greets me at the door and snuggles herself against my legs. It's a heartwarming feeling, a sensation that I would do anything to have.

I started to sketch out myself on my paper, erasing just about everything. Anything I drew looked crummy and not good enough.

I snuck a peek at the paper of the boy who sat next to me. What's his name? Elias, I think. I already forgot.

His paper was already a masterpiece, one deserved to be placed in some type of hall of fame. My mouth dropped open in awe. Everything he drew so far looked perfect.

From what I could see, there were two boys who were posing together for a selfie. They looked oddly familiar, too. Apparently, it was Elias and his friend, who sat next to him.

His drawing is a million times better than mine.

I turned back to mine, raising an eyebrow at the eraser marks that smeared through the paper. I guess I put too much force in trying to sketch. Oops.

I started to sketch out Cookie and I, sketching as slowly, but efficiently as I could. By the time about ten minutes rolled around, the bell rang, signaling that school is over for the day.

My drawing doesn't look that bad, but it isn't decent, either. My arms, my head, and Cookie's paws look weird. Unfortunately, they were the most noticeable things anyone could see, too. However, since this is a pre-test, and this isn't for a grade, the way my drawing looks doesn't matter.

"Okay everyone, before you leave, put your drawings at the middle of your table neatly. I'll collect them soon," Ms. Edwards announced, clapping her hands together. "Class is dismissed. I'll see you all tomorrow."

I placed my pencil in the side pocket of my backpack. I took out a book I borrowed from the public library and hugged it against my chest. I'm not going to read it or anything. I'm just gonna hold it, especially since my backpack is stuffed with supplies.

I met Nora at the door of the classroom. We exited and started our journey to the student parking lot.

"Can you believe that we're seniors now?" Nora proclaimed with jazz hands. "We're at the tippy-top of the chain!"

"Yeah, it's hard to believe. It feels like we were freshmen not too long ago," I stated before climbing up the first step of a vacant stairway.

"I know, right? Time flies by quickly," she agreed, nodding her head.

I remember the first day of school as freshmen. Just like everyone else, I roamed the broad hallways of this school, wondering where to go. It feels like it happened yesterday. It's interesting how fast time can go.

But in the case of this school year, I think that it'll be a weird mix of fast and slow, especially slow since I'm dreading this school year. I'm almost completely sure that I'll make it. I mean, I made it through today. Just one-hundred seventy-nine days left to go. It won't be the easiest journey, but it won't be too hard.

It will be . . . average.

02. Memories

RYLIE

THE PIERCING SPUTTER of Nora's car made me jump as I fastened my seatbelt, placing my backpack on the floor in front of my feet.

Her Toyota Corolla from maybe ten years ago sometimes made an ear-splitting sound while starting. It sort of sounded like a constipated goat trying to run a race . . . whatever that would sound like.

"You should try to get your car fixed. The engine sounds strange," I stated, grimacing at the screech the car made while Nora pulled away from the parking lot, steering past students who were in the way.

"I know, but it will cost me a fortune to get this fixed. I don't have the money for that, believe me," Nora chuckled, not taking her eyes off of the road ahead of her. "And since the car drives fine itself, that's all that matters, right?"

"Right," I said, clutching my fingers together.

"So anyway, what are you going to wear to school tomorrow?" Nora asked curiously, her face lighting up.

I clutched my fingers together while raising my eyebrows. I have no idea what I'm going to wear. I never do. When it comes to choosing something to wear for school, I always choose something random (just as long as it somehow matches, of course).

"I don't know . . . I haven't decided yet," I answered, glimpsing out of the car window. There were only trees, grass, and roads that led to the one we're driving on.

Nothing special.

"I can help you decide. If you don't have anything you want to wear in your closet, we can take a trip to the mall and buy you some clothes and everything one day!" She exclaimed, doing jazz hands with only one hand, the other on the wheel. "It will be awesome."

"That sounds great. But for tomorrow, I'll just wear a plain T-shirt and jeans." I stated with a shrug.

"Alright. That sounds simple, yet cute," Nora said before making a sharp turn towards my neighborhood.

She drove through a couple of streets in the neighborhood, steering around cars that stood in the way of the road. The car came to a gradual stop as it approached my house.

I unbuckled my seatbelt and picked up my backpack, gently swinging it on my shoulder. I opened the door and reached my feet towards the ground.

"Bye, Nora. I'll see you tomorrow," I smiled.

"Bye bye, Ry. See you tomorrow," she proclaimed.

I shut the door as she waved at me before pulling off. I trudged through the driveway to the front porch. I pulled my house key from the side pocket of my backpack and stuck it inside the keyhole, twisting it after.

The door opened a few seconds later. I gently pushed it open and went inside. I closed the door shut behind me. Before I could go anywhere, I was stopped by something fuzzy.

It was Cookie.

She snuggled herself against me as she meowed. I bent down on the floor and petted her head with caution. I rose back up as Cookie laid down on her cat bed near the door.

"Mom, I'm home!" I called out, marching through the foyer to the living room.

Mom laid on the couch, scrolling through something on her phone while watching a Real Housewives spin-off on TV. As soon as she saw me, she placed her phone on the accent table in front of the couch and plastered a smile across her face with a gleam in her eyes.

"Rylie, you're here. How was your day at school?" She asked as her face lit up.

"It was fine," I replied bluntly.

"That's nice," she turned to the TV, engaged in the discussion that the ladies in Real Housewives were having.

"Mhm," I hummed to myself.

I wandered to the kitchen and headed towards the pantry. I gazed inside of it for a few moments, debating on whether I should eat classic potato chips or barbeque flavored chips.

Without a doubt, I snatched both of the small-sized bags off of the shelf, hugging them lightly against my chest as I shut the door of the pantry. I made a beeline to the stairs, climbing each step leisurely.

Why don't I have enough energy to do something as simple as climbing a stairway?

After a few moments of climbing the stairs, after what seemed like forever, I strutted down the hallway to my bedroom. As soon as I got in there, I set my backpack on the floor and collapsed onto the bed face first.

My room was dim, like usual. The blinds weren't open, even if there is way too much daylight out there. The room was so dark to the point where I couldn't see the black, heart-shaped stickers that were plastered on my wall.

Before I managed to open my two bags of chips, I pulled out my phone from the back pocket of my high-rise jeans. I pressed the home button to power it on, revealing a selfie of Nora and I on my home screen. We had our tongues stuck out as we did silly faces. The picture was from a few years ago, when we were thirteen or fourteen-years-old.

The picture brought back memories. It wasn't the picture itself that brought the memories. It was the time when the picture was taken. It wasn't the best time in my life, that's for sure.

It was filled with grief. Way too much, if you ask me.

I slouched up, setting my phone on my nightstand next to my lamp. I placed my hands over my cheeks, my elbows resting on my lap.

Sometimes, I wish I could completely forget about the past, like a hard drive being wiped out entirely. It's easier than said, for sure. There's always one thing, that's either big or small that will trigger memories . . . unpleasant ones.

My thoughts were interrupted by the sounds of footsteps coming close, along with a melodious hum of a song. It was Mom . . . and she's either coming here or to her room. Since I somehow left the door of my bedroom open, there's a large chance she'll stop by to check on me.

"Rylie, are you alright?" Mom questioned with concern, cradling Cookie in her arms. "You look pale."

I knew it.

"I'm fine, Mom," I plastered a fake smile across my face, setting my hands on my lap.

"Are you sure? I can tell that something is . . . off," she raised an eyebrow, setting Cookie on the floor.

Cookie strutted to me and jumped on my bed. I hugged her against my chest, stroking the warm tan fur on her head.

"Yes, I'm sure," I lied, keeping my focus on Cookie who squirmed in my arms.

"If you say so. But if you're not, you should probably get some fresh air or something," Mom suggested with a hopeful smile before traveling down the hall to her bedroom.

She is right. I do need some fresh air. But believe me, not from outside. I need to get out and try to avoid overthinking. There's one place that will provide a perfect distraction.

The public library. Crews City Public Library to be exact.

I snatched my phone off my nightstand and grabbed my almost overdue books I borrowed from the library. I strutted to the foot of my bed and picked up a mini-backpack, one I often carry when I go out somewhere.

I placed my phone and the books in the mini-backpack with caution, then closed it with the zipper. I placed the straps on my shoulder. I put the two bags of chips I never got to eat in my bag, as well. Before I abandoned my bedroom, I gave Cookie a brief hug and filed out the door. I rushed down the flight of stairs and approached the front door.

"Mom, I'm going to the library," I hollered loud enough for her to hear.

"Okay. Be back here in an hour or so!" She stated.

"Bye," I said before closing the door behind me as I left.

Ten minutes after I arrived at the library, I made my journey towards the back of the library, where it was most silent and idle. I sat at a table in the corner, perfect enough for my liking. I set my bag on a chair, while I sat in the one next to it.

A copy of The Fault in Our Stars laid in my hands. I've read the novel five times, believe me. I can never get enough of reading the story. It's... spectacular. I'm not gonna spoil the story, but it's amazing, despite the countless amount of times I cried while reading the book.

I grabbed my earbuds and phone from the front pocket of my bag. I turned on my phone and went straight to Spotify. Without any doubt, I tapped on a playlist I made filled with pop songs. It will hopefully help my mind drift off as I read.

I shoved my earbuds in my ears, pressing the play button of my playlist. Blank Space by Taylor Swift blasted. I can somehow find myself relating to the song in some type of way.

Next, No Tears Left To Cry by Ariana Grande blared through the speakers of my earbuds. Yet another song I could find myself somehow relating to in a way. Especially the title. I always feel that I want to be happy after a long time of feeling under the weather. But in my case, I don't know how.

I sighed as I turned to the first page in The Fault in Our Stars, recognizing each word I read immediately. Without taking my attention off the book, I reached towards my bag, opened it, and took one of the two bags of chips I brought.

I chose the classic potato chips. Perfect.

Believe it or not, I have strong passion for the two flavors. They're both something I'd eat anytime, anywhere. But right now, I'm sort of more in the mood for something salty . . . and potato chips are ideal for that.

I opened the bag of chips, reaching my hand into the bag. I shoved a chip in my mouth, savoring the salty and crunchy taste of it.

As time passed, my mind began to drift off . . . not in the way I wanted it to. I began to reflect on my life, and how it was filled with events that made a change . . . one that isn't good. I've probably thought about it a billion times. I have forever been needing to get everything off my chest . . . but I don't know how, or who to talk to.

Not like anyone would truly understand my burning pain, anyway.

03. Competition

ELIAS

"YOU SHOULDN'T WALK and draw at the same time," Cannon suggested with a facepalm I could see with the corner of my eye. "You might bump into something . . . or someone."

It's already the second day of school and I'm already sketching random lines in the back of one of my notebooks. During my entire high school experience so far, I've been sketching in notebooks and loose papers whenever I feel bored in school, which clearly is right now.

Ayden "Cannon" Daniels, my best friend, has always been there to warn me not to do so. Of course, I always find a way to do the opposite. We've been friends for as long as I remember. Maybe kindergarten or first grade. We became friends just by speaking with each other. During lunch, we traded sandwiches our mothers made for us. During recess, we drew whatever we could think of on the sidewalk outside our school with chalk.

Cannon always gave off bright vibes, like colors on a rainbow that reflect throughout sunlight. He almost always found a light through everything, no matter how dark it may be.

Now that we're seniors in high school, it's time to be a bit more serious about everything, starting with me not sketching something on whatever paper I could find.

"I know I shouldn't walk and draw at the same time, Cannon," I chuckled, closing the cover of my spiral notebook. "I just can't help it."

"I get that, but when you bump into someone or something, don't say I didn't warn you," he tutted.

"I won't," I said before stuffing my notebook into my backpack.

If I hadn't put away my notebook, I probably visually wouldn't have noticed that we were almost at the cafeteria for lunch. People crowded through the doors, chatting and joking with each other loudly with each other. Cannon and I squeezed our way through the doors, making a beeline towards the back. The smell of freshly cooked food prickled my nose, automatically causing my stomach to roar.

We joined the line, which only had a few people in it for the time being. I reached to the front pocket of my backpack, rummaging through everything in it to see if I could find a few dollars. There was my tangled earbuds and crumpled sticky notes filled with random sketches, but no money. Not even a penny. I should've made sure I had a few dollars in my backpack this morning, but I guess I forgot.

"Cannon, can I borrow five dollars? I forgot my money at home," I questioned, clutching my fingers together. "I'll pay you back tomorrow."

"Of course you can have some money, Eli," Cannon tutted, reaching towards the pocket of his bright blue jeans. He fished a five dollar bill out of it. "Don't worry about paying me back."

"Thank you so much," I accepted the dollar from his hand.

"No problem," he said, gesturing towards the moving line in front of us.

It's now my turn to order what I want for lunch. The food they serve here at Crews isn't the best, but it isn't the worst. Overall, I'd rather order something to eat from a restaurant or grab something from home instead of eating food from here, but that isn't possible right now. I requested for a hamburger, fries, apple slices, along with a water bottle. The lunch lady that worked at the register charged me four dollars and fifty cents. It's the perfect price, considering that I only have five dollars.

I handed her the money and she gave me my change before stuffing it into my back pocket. I grasped my fingers tightly against my tray, stepping aside a bit to allow the lunch line to move on. After Cannon paid for his meal, we strutted across the cafeteria, searching for an empty table to sit at. The only idle table that we could see was near the large windows . . . which is also where the trash cans are. The unpleasant odor of the trash cans invaded the area, along with a few flies that buzzed around. Gross.

"How do you like senior year so far, Eli?" Cannon asked, combing a hand through his shaggy, lemonade-pink hair.

"It's been fine," I replied, lifting the bun of my burger. There was only a few drops of ketchup, making the burger look ordinary. "What about you?"

"Mines have been all over the place, but nothing bad. I think I'm interested in one guy in our History class, the one with raven hair that always rests over his honey eyes," he put his hand over his chest, disappointment growing in his voice. "But then, I found out that he's straight and has a girlfriend. I swear, he was so adorable!"

"Bummer," I replied, my disappointment matching his.

"It is. I'm tired of being single . . . I'm so, so ready to mingle," he sighed, poking his fork through the salad he ordered.

Ever since Cannon came out a few years ago, all he ever wanted was a friendly boy that would love him just as much as he would.

"You'll just have to keep waiting for the right time to come," I assured him.

"I know," Cannon mustered a smile, followed by a smirk. "Anyway, what about you? Do you have eyes for anyone yet?"

"Uh, no. Not yet," I answered, biting a piece of an apple slice.

"Alright," he chuckled.

I don't have any type of crush or whatever with anyone here at school. Not yet, at least. Even if I did have a crush on someone, I'm sure that there's a large chance that they won't like me back.

For now, that's fine since I don't like anyone in that way. After all, I want to focus on school—specifically art. This year, I want to work extra hard in that class and participate in any art contest that our school might have. Art is my passion, especially painting. It's my way of escaping reality. When I get older, I want to become an artist. It's the only thing I can imagine myself being.

Of course, my parents don't think the same.

Ever since they found out that I wanted to be an artist a few years ago, they've tried to discourage me countless times, saying that I should be someone that is considered something—whatever that means, like a doctor or a lawyer. There's nothing wrong with those jobs, but they're just not for . . . me.

Entering a popular art contest at school and winning it might change my parents minds. If I'm that good at art to win—or at least come in second or third place—their perspective on me wanting to become an artist might change.

IN THE BOOKS

The most popular art contest that I know of here is The Crews City Visual Art competition, TCVA, which usually opens late September, and closes in December. The contest will open in several weeks from now. I've already made the decision to enter when my artwork will be finished, whenever that will be.

The sound of a deafening laugh interrupted my thoughts as it neared closer to me. Axel Hanson strutted by our table, shooting a soda can into one of the trash bins behind us. Before he could get back to his table—which is somewhere in the middle of the lunchroom, he stopped to talk to someone, while eyeing me suspiciously.

Why is Axel fucking Hanson looking at me like that?

Before anyone can make any assumptions, he and I aren't rivals. Well, in most ways we aren't. We're just competitive when it comes to art. For the entire time we've been in high school, we've pretty much done everything we could to determine who's the better at art—me or him. Yes, I know; it's unnecessary and pointless. But I guess we can't help it.

Axel began to walk away from where he was, separating from the person he was talking to to join his girlfriend, Adrienne Griffin.

They've been dating for three and a half years, longer than most of the relationships a lot of people here at Crews had. As they strutted away, Axel threw a playful but stern smirk at me, his mocha brown eyes somehow giving me chills.

Between Axel and me competing over everything related to art and myself willing to do my best in art class, this year is gonna be a long, yet interesting year.

Throughout all my four years at Crews High School, Ms. Edwards has always been my favorite teacher. Not because she teaches my favorite subject. It's because of how friendly, creative, and open-minded she is. Her class is the class I was interested in most. Her class is the only class where I can be myself, and do what I adore.

Today in her class, we're learning about realistic still life drawing. I already knew some of the things she went over, but a few things were oddly new to me. After Ms. Edwards modeled what to do, she gave us all paper to practice a few of the sketching strokes she went over, as well as some shapes.

Easy stuff.

"I can't wait until we actually start drawing our still life drawings," Cannon squealed like someone who just saw a baby animal or human.

"Me too. I hope I get an A on it," I gleamed, stroking my pencil across my paper to draw a circle.

"Same here," Axel added from out of the blue. He sits across from me in this class. It's exactly what I need to focus on my work. Not.

His smirk broadened as he stared at me, as if we were having a stare down. I let out a sigh as I let go of my pencil. After staring at each other for what seemed like forever, Axel finally turned back to his paper, and I did the same.

When class ended about twenty minutes later, Ms. Edwards called Axel and I up to her desk to discuss something before we would go home.

"Hi, Ms. Edwards," Axel gleamed.

"Hi," I said with a wave. "What did you need us for?"

"I just wanted to tell you all great news," Ms. Edwards beamed, putting a strand of her strawberry-blonde hair behind her ear while viewing something on her laptop. "The date of TCVA has been planned. The contest will start on September twenty-third. Since you two are the best at art in this class period, I decided to tell you this early in case you'd be interested."

"That's awesome," I could see Axel wink at me from the corner of my eye. "Perfect."

"Yeah, that's great," I added.

"Mhm. I know that you two will do great if you decide to enter," Ms. Edwards smiled.

Since the contest will start soon, everything will change between Axel and I. We'll be a lot more competitive than we are right now.

Being competitive about something some people would consider little is unnecessary, but for me, it's for a good cost. I want to convince my parents that being an artist is considered a great thing. I want them to be proud of me. As of now, the only way I could do that is to enter and win TCVA. But of course, Axel is going to make everything harder than it should be.

This school year will indeed be interesting.

04. It Pours

RYLIE

DROPS OF RAIN beaded down the roof to the window, dripping on the outer window sill. The crisp aroma of the rainfall invaded my bedroom spread from the open window. Crisp wind blew against my wavy curls that blew behind my ears. I've always enjoyed the rain. The way it pattered against the roof was satisfying, the way it smelled was pleasing, and the way it sounded was gratifying.

Rainy days are also a perfect excuse for me to stay inside the house and sulk. My mother insists that it isn't good for me—and I know she's right—but I can't help it. Today, I don't have the inspiration to do anything else.

I took a deep breath before abandoning the desk chair I sat on near the window. I placed my phone and house keys inside the pocket of my black hoodie. Before I could take one last look at my window, Cookie stopped me dead in my tracks and meowed, as if she was asking what was the matter.

I picked her up with my arms and hugged her lightly, scratching behind her ears with my hand. She purred, followed by another meow. I guess she wants an answer.

"I'm fine, Cookie. It's just that . . . I don't feel good today," I replied with a sigh, plopping myself on the rim of my bed, only causing her to meow. "I'd say more if my answer isn't enough for you, but I don't want to traumatize you."

It's true. Today is a day where I feel off. I can blame it all on today's date, September sixteenth. This day may mean absolutely nothing to some people, but to me, it means everything—and it's all for a reason. Cookie meowed once again and leapt off of my bed and stretched herself, snuggling on the floor before falling asleep. My lips pursed into a smile, then faded back into the way it was before—a glower.

I sighed heavily before opening the door of my bedroom, racing out of the room. I proceeded down the hall to the staircase, carefully walking down each step. Once I reached the bottom, I headed towards the front door, opened it, walked out, and closed the door behind me. I'm not going to go anywhere anyone would think I would go. I'm going to go somewhere nearly nobody would go, especially on a rainy day like today.

The cemetery.

Yes, the cemetery. They've always creeped me out. Not only because there were dead people dug into the ground, but because of its creepy vibes. The way the wind howled, blowing against the leaves on nearby trees was terrifying. The creak the gates of the graveyard made whenever it opened or closed was disturbing.

Everything about the graveyard is . . . off.

But today, I'm going to go there, especially since Mom isn't home and won't come home from work for another two hours or something. She might ask questions that I may not want to answer. Don't get me wrong. I'm not going to the graveyard to mope around and stare at the ground. I'm going there to visit someone, a person who means a lot to me.

My thoughts were interrupted by the howl of the wind that covered the gentle sound of the rain that patted across the paved ground. It wasn't a lot, but it was enough to the point where I was already soaked. I should've brought an umbrella with me. I guess I was too drenched in my thoughts to even remember to bring one.

"Shit," I heard myself mumble under my breath, pulling my hoodie over my head a few centimeters more. Rain dripped on my hoodie, as well as my shoes as I trudged inches closer to the graveyard. I could go back home to grab an umbrella, but there's no point in that now. I'm already here at the cemetery and I'm not turning back . . . even if I want to.

I laid my hand on the handle of the cemetery's aged metal gate. Water dripped from the sides of it, cascading down my hand to my wrist. I shook it off as I pulled the gate open, leaving a space large enough for me to proceed to the actual cemetery. The gate creaked in an obnoxious, yet spooky sound that made my spine chill.

Believe me, it's terrifying.

I stepped in a small puddle of water before I walked over the lush, fern-green grass. I made a sharp turn to the left area of the graveyard, observing each and every grave before stopping at one. This grave had Asher Colton Henderson engraved over it.

Asher Colton Henderson.

Yes, we're related. In fact, he's my dad.

When I was a young child, we had a strong connection. I could never imagine myself passing a day without seeing him. Of course, I still adored my mom—but I liked my dad better for some reason. We went to the park together, got ice cream together, and even went on picnics together, along with Mom. Our connection was one that I wanted to last forever. Unfortunately, it didn't. It only lasted a few years more.

When I was ten or eleven years old, everything changed. It was like everything began to tumble down hard, like bricks or heavy stones. It all started with Mom and Dad bickering over anything and everything. Whether it would be over a small thing or over something serious, it hurt me a lot. Sometimes, they would argue late into the night, refusing to be anywhere near each other. That left me to spend dozens of nights to wonder if they'd stay together.

At this time, we never got ice cream together anymore, or went to the park or on picnics. Yeah, I know; maybe I was outgrowing the park a bit, but still. It hurt a lot. My parents would always tell me that everything would be okay. Part of me wanted to believe them, but deep down, I knew that everything wouldn't be okay.

And I was correct.

When I was thirteen or fourteen, everything went downhill even more. My parents ended up filing for a divorce. When I found out, I was shocked, but at the same time, under the weather. Never in my life would I think that they would decide to split up. When I was younger, they could hardly stay away from each other. I was confused on how that could change . . . but it did. It somehow did.

From that point on, all I wanted to do was hide in my room and ponder on how our little family of three would become. I knew that it wouldn't be good, but in reality, it became worse than I thought. Dad ended up packing up all his things and moving out of our house to an apartment that wasn't far from where we stayed. It felt weird to not have him in the house. It was oddly . . . quiet.

At the time, I sort of lost touch with him. By that, I mean that our connection went downhill. We hardly talked over the phone or in-person. We sometimes sent postcards to each other, but not often. I guess the same could be said about Mom and I, even if the two of us didn't have a connection as close as Dad's and mine.

I felt nothing but isolated and fatigued, not to mention that this all happened during the summer break before I started ninth grade. When the school year started, all I wanted to do was talk to no one. I wasn't interested in going to school events or group work. I didn't even want to join the school's reader's rally, which I'd sign up for the second it would be announced back in middle school.

All I wanted to do was go to school, do my work, and go home—or even better—stay at home and sulk (which my mother refused to let me do). One or two weeks later, an unexpected person came to the door of our house. It was an officer, and he came to break some bad news to us. It was news that would change our lives forever.

The officer told us how Dad got into a severe car accident. Those few words were enough to make me break down into tears, but that wasn't it. The officer also told us that he was found drunk, which was oddly surprising since I would never imagine my father to drink and drive at the same time. The last thing the officer told us was that he didn't survive.

As soon as I heard those words that day—September sixteenth—I sobbed, harder than I ever had before. The divorce between my parents was already enough to tire me out, and the heartbreaking news made matters worse. I remember that my mom was trying to console me, but none of it worked. I ended up crying for the rest of the day and didn't sleep for the entire night.

I felt as if my heart had been broken into multiple pieces. At that point, I didn't want to do anything. I didn't want to go anywhere or speak to anyone. I only wanted my dad to be alive and my parents to be together and happy. It was a wish that was never going to come true.

Tears trickled down the corner of my eyes, rolling down my cheeks to the tip of my chin. I wiped as many tears as I could with the back of my hand. Soon enough, my hand wasn't doing enough about the tears that kept falling from my eyes. It was like I was crying a storm—one that won't stop anytime soon.

"Hey," a familiar voice said from meters away. "Are you alright? You look soaked from the rain."

My head turned to face whoever was there. It was Elias from school. He had a scarlet-red umbrella that shielded his head, protecting him from the rain. A warm smile danced across his lips, covering the concern in his eyes.

I can't let him see me crying—it will be embarrassing. I began to wipe my face so I could look presentable. I managed to keep in some tears, but it won't last long.

"I'm fine," I muttered with a sniff. "Why are you here?"

"I was walking home, but I saw you standing here from the fence of this place," Elias replied, gesturing to the rusted, bronze fence that was behind us. "I didn't realize it was you at first, but I came here anyway just to make sure you're okay. You don't have an umbrella or anything and it's raining a lot."

"Oh. It may be raining, but I'm fine," I insisted, looking him in the eye.

"Okay," Elias muttered, adjusting his umbrella. "You're Rylie from art at school, right?"

"Yeah," I stared at the ground, brushing a foot against the grass.

"Cool," he replied. "You can borrow my umbrella. I think you need it more than me."

He was right. My entire self is soaked with water, especially my hoodie. I'm also beginning to smell musky. I may like the rain, but I don't like this feeling. It's weird.

"But if I borrow your umbrella, then you'll get wet," I reasoned. "I don't want that to happen."

"It's fine. My house isn't far from here. Plus, I'll run," Elias insisted, handing the handle of the umbrella to me.

I hesitantly accepted it and hovered the umbrella over my head. It was quite a relief to not feel rain drops splatter all over me.

"Thank you for letting me borrow it," I muttered, plastering a small smile across my face. "I'll give it back to you tomorrow at school."

"No problem. By the way, why are you here?" He questioned.

"I'm only here to visit someone," I stated, hoping that he wouldn't ask why. "You should get going now. Your starting to get soaked from the rain yourself."

"You're right," he said, putting the hood from his hoodie over his head. "I'll see you tomorrow at school."

He waved his hand before walking away to the gate of the cemetery. I watched him leave before he disappeared out of sight. I gripped the handle of his umbrella tightly. If Elias never came to the cemetery to let me borrow his umbrella, I would've still been here, soaked with water.

I faced my attention towards my father's grave, giving it one last look before strutting towards the gate of the cemetery. I let out the tears that I managed to hold back while Elias was here. Being in this cemetery is only making me feel sad—sadder than I already am.

"I miss you, Dad," I said solemnly before abandoning his grave.

Mom was the first thing I saw when I arrived home. Her arms were folded against her chest. She looked at me as if she asked me a question, and I didn't have an answer.

"Uh . . . Hi, Mom," I muttered, plastering a fake smile across my face.

"Hi, Rylie," she said, her arms still crossed. "I've been wondering where you've been since I got home from work a few minutes ago."

"I was at the cemetery," I explained briefly. "And I thought you were going to come home in at least two hours or something."

"I finished my work, so I decided to come home early," she stated, motioning me towards the living room. "Even when I'm not here, you should always tell me where you're going if you decide to go somewhere by text or something."

I nodded my head up and down. Mom doesn't like when I go places without telling her first. It makes her anxious. I'll definitely keep that in mind.

I sat on one of the arm chairs of our living room, while Mom sat on the sofa. She was still in her work clothes, which was an berry blue blazer dress and heels the same color to match.

"You look like you've been crying," Mom broke the silence while glimpsing at my face. "Is it because of the cemetery?"

"Well, yeah. It's just because of my memories with Dad. Looking at his grave made me break down into tears," I sniffed, glimpsing down at the tan, wooden floor.

"I know you're sad about it. I am too, and seeing you in pain makes me sadder," she sighed. "You've been holding everything in for the past four years or so. I think you should talk to some type of therapist to let everything out."

"I don't want to go to a therapist, Mom," I groaned. "I don't want to talk to some stranger about my problems."

"Then what about a teen support group? I hear they have one in town, and it's for free. It'll help you, sweetie," Mom suggested. "They have them every Tuesday and Thursday."

How in the world is a teen support group going to help me? I'm sure it will basically be me telling a group of strangers about how I feel, and I don't see the point in that.

"Do I have to go there?" I questioned sluggishly. "I don't want to go."

"I can't force you, but I don't like seeing you like this. It hurts me a lot. Please try to go," she pleaded.

The pleading look on her face started to make me feel kind of bad. If I say no, then she'll be unhappy and I'll feel guilty. Even if I don't want to go to the support group, I'll go anyway. I don't see how it'll help me, but I guess it's worth a try.

05. Baby Steps

RYLIE

AFTER SCHOOL TODAY, Mom picked me up and drove me to the building where the teen support group takes place. It's only been a day since she has recommended that I come here. I agreed to come today, only so I could get this over with.

We pulled up at a large, two-story building that was erected tall against the sky. Originally, I imagined the teen support group in a small, crampy building. But no, it appears that it's in a building that provides health and mental health services for our city.

I anxiously looked at the front of the building, staring at the mocha brown brick wall. I'm not looking forward to going to this support group. The thought of telling strangers about my problems gives me chills. Despite every bit of me wanting to skip going to the support group, I'm going to go, mainly because it'll make Mom happy.

"I'll come back here in an hour to pick you up," she stated, pulling in for a hug. "I'm proud of you for taking a big step to come here. It'll be good for you. Love you."

"I love you too, Mom," I said, wiggling myself free from her hug.

I exited the car and shut the door, waving at her on the edge of the sidewalk. She waved back before she pulled off. I sighed, turning myself to look at the building. I have no choice but to go inside. I went through the automatic doors, my eyes focused on the navy blue hue of the walls, along with a few colorful posters that pointed directions to where everything was. A receptionist who sat behind a desk, flashing a smile at me once she saw me come in.

"Hello, how can I help you?" She asked genuinely, adjusting the rim of her glasses with her fingers.

"I'm here for the teen support group. Do you know where it is?" I told her, staring down at the denim, blue carpet.

"Yes, just sign this paper first," she placed a clipboard and pen on the desk, sliding it towards my direction. "The support group is upstairs.

Take the elevator down this hall, go to the left, and you'll see the support group in room twelve to the right."

"Thanks," I said, signing my signature on the paper before returning it to her.

I strutted down the hall towards the elevator, glimpsing at the frames that contained photos of happy children and adults on them. I gently pressed the elevator button with my finger and tapped my foot against the ground. I don't want to be here, I really don't. I just want to be home in the comfort of my room. But Mom says otherwise.

The doors of the elevator creaked open as the bell rang. Even if the door was open, I didn't go inside. My feet stayed put to the ground, as if they were attached to it with glue. Before the doors had a chance to close, I rushed inside and practically hit the upper level button. The doors closed, and a few seconds later, I could hear the roaring motor of the elevator move. The sooner I go to this support group, the sooner I can leave.

When the elevator doors bolted open, I rushed out and turned left, just like the receptionist told me. I wandered down the hall, examining each door I could see on the right side of the corridor. Once I reached room twelve, I hesitantly peeked my head through the door frame. I thought that doing that would make no one notice me. But apparently, I'm wrong. A lady that looked like she was in her mid-thirties smiled at me. I guess she's the counselor for this support group program.

I plastered a fake smile across my face as I tip-toed into the room. Other than the counselor, there were four other teens in the room. They all had their arms crossed and looked like they'd rather be somewhere else, just like me.

All the chairs in the room were set up in a circle, spaced from each other by a few inches. I sat on the one that was one chair away from the counselor. Then, I crossed my arms while tapping my feet against the ground. Other than the noise of me tapping my feet, the room was silent to the point where I could hear the clock on the wall ticking. The wall was plain white, which strangely made the room seem a bit bigger than it was.

"It looks like everyone is here," the counselor stated with a warm smile. "I see a new face." She turned to me, her broad smile not disappearing one bit. "I'm Leah, what's your name?"

"I-I'm Rylie," I muttered while clutching my fingers.

"Your name is pretty," Leah acknowledged. "I like it."

"Thanks, I guess," I said, glancing towards the door. "I'm going to go use the restroom. I'll be right back."

"Okay," she smiled, turning to another person. "The restroom is to the right when you go down the hall."

I rose up from my chair and trudged out of the room, wandering down the hall to look for the bathroom. In reality, I'm not actually going to use it. I'm just going to sit there for a few minutes. Once I spotted the ladies' restroom, I went inside, strutted to the nearest stall, and locked myself in there.

Nearly every part of me wanted to hide here for the remainder of the support group meeting. Being here makes me feel nervous. But if I skip the meeting, Mom will be disappointed and broken.

I don't want that to happen, so I guess I'll go back to the room where the support group takes place. I feel so many emotions about talking about my past to people. Part of me wants to do it to let it off my chest, but the other part of me just wants to keep it to myself. It's confusing and I have no clue what to do.

I need to figure it out . . . I just need to.

"How was it?" Mom questioned as I got in the car, instantly collapsing into the seat as I put on my seatbelt.

The support group ended a few minutes ago. I feel nothing but grateful that it did because I felt like I couldn't be in that building any longer. I ended up not speaking up about my past during the meeting. Leah asked if I wanted to say something, but I refused politely. Mom won't be happy about this if she finds out. I'm sure she will if she asks me.

"The support group was fine, I guess," I muttered.

"Did you participate in it?" She asked, glimpsing at me before looking back at the road ahead of us.

I knew it.

"Uh . . ." I bit my lip. "Yes . . ?"

"Are you sure?" She squinted her eyes, suspicious appearing in her voice. "Something tells me that you're lying."

"I'm sure," I tried to sound as honest as I could.

"Nice try, Rylie, but I know that you're lying. I can see it in your face," Mom sighed.

Great. Now Mom knows that I didn't do anything at the support group. That's the last thing I wanted to happen. I guess I'm a bad liar, or Mom is good at catching simple lies. Maybe both. Lying isn't good either way, but in this case, I just had to do it.

"You're right . . ." I let out a deep breath.

"Why didn't you say anything? If you at least let one little thing out, it would've helped you," she stated. "Keeping everything in isn't good for you."

"I know, but I don't know what to do," I clutched my fingers. "I want to talk about it, but it'll be hard. Plus, I feel like no one will understand. I feel alone."

"That's what the support group is for. The counselor will understand. The other teenagers there have similar problems, so you won't feel alone," Mom assured me, extending her arm for it to rest on my shoulder.

"I guess you're right," I murmured.

All this talking distracted me so much to the point where I didn't realize that we're already on the driveway of home.

"I have some groceries in the trunk. Can you help me put them inside and put them away?" Mom questioned, opening her door of the car to exit.

"Sure," I said, opening my door to abandon the car.

If I said no, Mom would start complaining how I do nothing around the house or something. It isn't true, but she'll find a reason to still say that. Mom opened the trunk with her car keys and I grabbed two bags with my hands. There were only four bags in the trunk, so I'll let her carry the other two. The garage door was open, so I went through there to go inside. I placed the bags on the white, fake granite countertop.

As soon as Mom came in, her phone started to ring from her purse. She placed the groceries on the countertop and fished her phone out of her purse.

"I have to take this call," she said, glancing at the screen of her phone with a coy smile. "Can you put the groceries away?"

"Okay . . ." I answered, raising an eyebrow.

Mom disappeared into the living room to go to the foyer. I shrugged as I took the groceries out of their bags one-by-one. I placed an egg carton into its designated place in the refrigerator, along with the milk. I don't mind putting away groceries. It's just something that I don't like to do.

I sighed as I thought about today, specifically the support group. I feel kind of bad for not participating, only because that's what Mom wanted me to do. Even if I think that the support group won't help me, I still could've tried to say something. Not anything big. I could've just given a brief description of what happened. Maybe if I take baby steps, I can gradually feel better.

I guess it's worth a try when I'm ready.

06. Pressure

ELIAS

WORKING AT A restaurant isn't the easiest job.

Believe me, it isn't. I've been working at one for a year now and I've witnessed and dealt with plenty of angry customers. I'm only a crew member—which is someone who takes orders, processes payments, and prepares food. I mostly only take orders and process payments, but working at a fast food restaurant is quite a job.

And unfortunately, I'm going to work today.

The only reason I have it is so I can pay for all the art supplies I want. My parents don't give me money to buy art supplies, mainly because they think it's pointless and stuff. I don't mind paying for things on my own, especially since I'm seventeen and going to turn eighteen soon. It's just that my parents don't see how being an artist is the only thing I want to be when I am older.

I've heard them say those words a million times, and I don't want to hear it ever again.

I picked up my aged sketchpad and pencil from my desk and hugged them against my chest with one hand, while the other grabbed my backpack from the floor. My work uniform is already on, so I'm good to go. Before I left my room, I took one last look at it.

The three paintings I painted not too long ago highlighted the beige color of the walls. One painting was one of me, the second one was Mom, Dad, and I together, and the third one was of Cannon and I. They haven't seen the paintings just yet, but when they do, I wonder what their reaction will be.

I walked out the door and headed towards the stairs. After successfully climbing down each step, I headed towards the living room. Mom and Dad were on the couch watching some type of movie on the flat-screen TV.

"I'm going to work now. See you in a few hours," I proclaimed, gripping my sketchbook tightly.

"Okay," Mom glimpsed at me with a smile.

"See you later, son," Dad added. "Also, we saw the paintings in your room today when you went to school. We're very impressed."

My face lit up as my mouth dropped open. Trying to impress my parents with my art has been what I wanted to do for so long. But to not keep my hopes up too much, what if they're not impressed enough? What if they still think that I shouldn't become an artist?

"Since you're impressed, do you think that I'd become a great artist when I'm older?" I questioned as I clutched my fingers nervously.

At this point, who knows what their answer will be. I'm too terrified to know the answer to the point where my spine is sort of starting to chill.

"I don't know, Elias. It's just that in the future, you need to get a good job that pays well," Dad replied.

"But what if I don't enjoy doing a job that pays well?" I asked, stuffing my sketchbook into my backpack.

"Life isn't about enjoying things, unfortunately. You have to work very hard once you're an adult. Being something big when you're older will help you," Mom stated. "Being an artist won't guarantee you making a decent amount of money to put a roof over your head."

I've heard these words a million times already. If not, a billion. Maybe they're right when it comes to certain things they say. In the end, all I want is to do is become an artist full time. It may not guarantee to get me enough money to have a roof over my head, but I can always learn.

By the time senior year is over, I'll major in visual arts when college rolls around. The college I'll be going to—R. L. Laurier University—which isn't too far from where I am. Originally, I wanted to go to an art school, but my parents unsurprisingly won't pay for it. But that's fine, I guess. I can still do decent at Laurier.

Once I brush up my art skills—specifically painting—I can prove Mom and Dad wrong. I can prove to them that being an artist—or anything that they would consider "small"—can make you enough money to put a roof over your head. I know that I'll have to work my ass off to succeed. It'll be hard to juggle between family, friends, school—and later life, but it has to be done.

I let out a sigh as I strutted out of the living room, heading towards the front door in the foyer. It's three twenty-three and I'm supposed to be at work in seven minutes. Thinking can be a major distraction.

Taco Fiesta, the restaurant chain I work at, is only five minutes away from here. The restaurant has never been too busy or crowded, so I'm sure that I won't get into trouble if I somehow end up being a minute late or so.

As soon as I reached the entrance of my neighborhood, I rounded the corner down the sidewalk. The noises of cars and trucks rushing by blared loudly. The strong scent of a thick cloud of gas that came out of a freight truck stung my nose. I strolled down the sidewalk, spotting the large sign of Taco Fiesta. I began to jog, only because it's three twenty-nine. Once I reached the restaurant, I let out a deep breath as I trudged through the aged parking lot. It's been about five years since it's been paved or something.

When I reached the establishment, I pulled the handle of the door. The aroma of chili, tacos, burritos, tamales, and other similar foods welcomed me inside. The tiny sombreros and maracas on the wallpaper of the walls lit up the macaroon yellow tint the walls, along with colorful ribbon decorations.

I marched to the back area to enter the area behind the front desk. I strutted to the break room area to drop off my backpack. Before I left, I grabbed my Taco Fiesta baseball cap shaped hat and placed it on my head. I headed towards the front area while clutching my hands together. There was hardly anyone in the restaurant. There was only one customer who was seated at a booth, quietly munching on a burrito, and a few staff members.

This restaurant has fewer customers as time goes by. People usually prefer going to popular rather than small ones. Taco Fiesta is indeed one of them. The establishment is owned by a genuine couple in their late forties—Miguel and Isabella Mercado. I've known them since I was little. Whenever I came to this shop with my parents to purchase a taco, I never left unsatisfied. Their tacos were always juicy and mouthwatering. I sometimes don't understand why more people don't come here. Everything here is just . . . chef's kiss.

"Elias, hi!" Mr. Mercado greeted me, wiping sweat from his forehead with an aged, porcelain cloth.

"Good afternoon, Mr. Mercado," I smiled, gripping my hands on the countertop while facing him. "It's not a busy day, isn't it?"

"It's not. We've had some people come in but not much," he sighed.

"I'm sure more people will come," I reassured him with a warm smile.

"I hope so," Mr. Mercado said, returning my smile back.

He walked off into the kitchen area, joining a few other staff members who were sitting around with nothing to do. Without customers, all there is to do is sit around. I gripped my fingers against the counter, looking towards the front door of the restaurant. The bell attached to the door rang as the customer who was seated at the booth left. Moments later, the bell rang again as the door flung open.

There wasn't just a random person at the door—it was Cannon. His hands were dug into his pockets as he strutted up to the counter, a coy grin spread across his face.

"Eli, hey!" his voice sounded energetic.

"Hi, Cannon. Can I get you anything?" I offered, my energy matching his.

"Yeah," he glanced at the large menu overhead. "Can I have two crunchy classic tacos with extra sour cream and a small orange Fanta?"

"Yes, that'll be four dollars and thirty cents," I typed everything into the register.

He foiled his hand into his pocket to reach out for his wallet. He grabbed a five dollar bill and slid it on the counter. "Here you go."

"Thanks," I said as I put the money into the cash register. I took out seventy cents and handed it to him. He accepted it and stuffed it into his pocket, along with his wallet. "The food should be ready in a few minutes."

I printed out a receipt from the register and handed it to him, turning to my co-workers who were still lounging around. Two of them got up from a chair to wash their hands and put on gloves. Afterwards, they started working on Cannon's order. In the meantime, I grabbed a small cup and cap from the storage area under the counter and strutted to the soda fountain, inserting the cup under the designated nozzle.

Before I pushed the lever, I scooped a generous amount of ice into the cup from the cooler below the fountain. I pushed down on the lever as the carbonated drink poured out of the nozzle slowly, but steady. The sound of beef cooking pricked my ears, and the zesty aroma of it hit my nostrils. I licked my lips as if I could almost taste it. Maybe I should get a taco, quesadilla, or something like that after work. I feel a bit hungry, after all.

Since not a lot of people came here today, Mr. Mercado will be generous enough to let me have a few leftovers. This is probably one of the only perks this job has, along with being able to do what I want when there aren't any customers to serve. My thoughts were interrupted by soda cascading down my hand as I abruptly removed the cup from the soda fountain.

It let out a deafening noise as a result. With caution, I transferred the cup to the countertop next to the fountain and sealed the cap on. I took an individually wrapped straw with one hand and the cup with another and took them back to the register counter. I handed Cannon his drink to him with a grin.

"Thanks, Eli," he acknowledged, his olive green eyes meeting mine. "Also, how long is your shift for today?"

"It lasts until six thirty, three hours away," I replied, glancing at the taco-shaped clock fastened to the wall above the door meters ahead.

"Cool!" He said. A co-worker slid a paper bag on the counter. Cannon grabbed it and held it tightly before walking off to a table to eat. I trailed behind him, mainly so I can sit since I'm already tired of standing.

"You look tired," he looked up to me after digging his hand into his bag.

"I am. I just wanna go home and sleep," I rubbed my temples.

"Mood," Cannon hummed. "Get a nice sleep tonight. Tomorrow is a special day, anyway."

"What's happening tomorrow?" I questioned out of curiosity, my eyes widening.

"The Crews Visual Art contest. Remember?" He chuckled before taking a large bit of his first taco.

"Right! I guess I was tired to the point where I kind of forgot," I swept my hand across my forehead.

How could I forget? TCVA is the biggest and most-known contest I can possibly enter. I need to start thinking about what I should do for the competition. I'm obviously going to make a painting—but what will I paint in particular? I have a little bit of time to decide, but I'll try to figure it out before I start sketching out what I'm going to paint.

I need to make a painting that'll impress the judges for the contest. I need to work as hard as I can, all while dealing with everything else—like school, family, and friends. I need to win first place to gain whatever prize to prove my parents wrong.

07. Mixed Feelings

RYLIE

"IT'LL TAKE ME forever to save up for Kylie's new eyeshadow palette," Nora groaned, sharpening her pencil with her personal, hand-held sharpener.

For the past ten minutes, Nora has been blabbing on and on about make-up, perfume, and anything that can possibly be related to that. It's enough to distract me from focusing on my work, but that's fine. I'm practically struggling, anyway. Art class has been challenging so far, even after a few weeks of practicing various pencil strokes for our still art assignment we have to complete.

I've been drawing a flower vase—something basic—and it's been nothing but a challenge. It's been a struggle to even sketch out simple pencil strokes. It seems like everyone else at this table is doing better at their assignment than me. Nora seems to be doing pretty well, even while chattering about make-up.

"Don't you have a job or something that'll help you gather enough money to buy the palette?" I questioned, turning away from my paper to her.

"Well, yeah," her neutral expression faded into a grimace, "but I spent most of my money on clothes last month."

"Yeah, but if you save your money, you'll be able to get it. It can't be hard, right?" I assured her.

"It won't be, I hope," Nora stated with ambition. "I'm dying to try out the colors on Kylie's palette."

"The colors on her palette are truly to die for!" A lively voice sang. It was the guy who sat across from her, the one with the lemonade pink hair that was shaggy and done in a hair style similar to Harry Styles'. I think his name is Cannon or something. An energetic smile danced across his lips. It was probably the biggest smile I've seen in ages.

"I know right!" Nora nodded in agreement before blabbing about make-up with Cannon.

It looks like the two have something in common.

I turned back to my paper, grimacing at the mess that was on it. Eraser smudges invaded the paper, along with inferior pencil strokes. Everything seemed . . . inadequate. Maybe I'm just an amateur at this, but I'm sure if Ms. Edwards looked at my work, she'd give me less than a fifty. At this point, there is no way to get rid of the eraser smudges on my paper, or the faint lines that my eraser couldn't get rid of.

I have no choice but to get a new paper and trash this one. I groaned as I picked up my paper and balled it up. I rose up from my seat and strutted to the teacher's desk to request for a new one. My eyes couldn't stay off the porcelain, tiled ground that had hints of various paints splattered across it.

"Ms. Edwards . . . can you give me a new p-paper?" I muttered, tossing my old one into the waste bin beside her desk.

"Of course," she beamed, looking up from her laptop. She reached into a drawer under her desk and grabbed a piece of paper, extending her arm to hand it to me. "Here you go!"

"Thank you," I accepted it.

She nodded in acknowledgement as I turned back, strutting towards my seat. I practically collapsed into my stool. Cannon and Nora were still in deep conversation, while Elias and the guy next to Nora were diligently working on their assignment. I took a peek at Elias' paper. His drawing was nothing but perfection. It was a million times better than anything I can draw—if not, a billion more.

If I could learn a trick or two from him, I'd be a lot better at this.

I picked up my pencil from my paper, but dropped it again. It rolled to the edge of the table and made a clatter sound when it landed on the tiled floor. Before I could bend down and grab it, Elias reached to the ground to retrieve it—mainly because it landed next to his shoe.

"Here," he proclaimed, holding my pencil in his hand.

I accepted it from him with a nod of acknowledgement—which allowed me to sneak another peek at his work. It's like I'm gazing at a masterpiece right now. Seriously, how is he so good?

Nearly every ounce of me wants to compliment him, but once part of me is holding me back. He's working so diligently and has all his focus on his work. I don't want to interrupt him. I probably already did when my pencil fell. He probably thinks I'm a klutz or something, or maybe I'm overthinking. I should probably just compliment him and focus on my work.

"Wow, you're r-really good at this," I praised while clutching my fingers together anxiously. "How do you draw so well?"

His head shot up from his paper as a beam formed on his face. "Thank you. I've been drawing since I was little, and have been practicing ever since. Do you need any help?"

He looked down to my paper, noticing that it was blank. There wasn't a pencil mark in sight. I guess I can use some help.

"I can use some," I mustered a smile.

He nodded and reached down to his backpack. He hauled out a spiral notebook and pulled two pieces of paper from the back of it. He set one in front of me and the other in front of him. He began to model for me a few basic strokes step-by-step with his pencil. I observed closely, copying whatever he did on my paper when he finished modeling an example, following each step he showed me. It was basically the same thing Ms. Edwards did for us a week or two ago, but I guess I didn't understand.

"I think I'm good now. Thanks for the help," I acknowledged, pushing my example paper aside.

"No problem," he turned back to his work, examining where he left off.

After the end of the school day, I headed straight home to my bedroom and snuggled into my day pajamas. Overall, they weren't pajamas. They were just comfortable clothes I wear when I don't plan on going anywhere. They're plush like pillows. I'd wear them in public, but they don't match and there's a rip on the bottom area of my pants.

My homework is already finished, so all I have left to do is to relax, other than to start studying for a couple of classes. I plopped myself on my bed face-first with a groan, reaching one hand to one of my pillows to stuff it over my head. A few moments later, my phone rang—disturbing the peaceful, yet awkward silence of my bedroom.

I slouched up and reached for my nightstand, snatching my phone off of it. Scam Likely appeared on the screen. I groaned and instantly pressed the decline button, cupping my phone back on the nightstand. I was pretty comfortable before I got up to get my phone, but like usual, there's always something to interrupt a pleasant feeling, unfortunately.

Instead of going back into the position I was in a minute ago, I leapt off my bed and strutted to the door of my room. The door was wide open so I peeked my head out of the door before I sauntered into the vacant hall. I walked to the left towards Mom's bedroom. I haven't seen or heard from her since I came back home an hour and a half ago. She's been pretty quiet since I came back a few hours ago.

The door of her bedroom was slightly open, giving me the opportunity to slide in. She was nowhere in sight. I trudged to the bathroom and peeked my head through the side of the doorframe. Mom was humming to herself while applying scarlet red lipstick to her lips. She wore a cobalt blue dress and a golden necklace that was shaped like a flower, which I knew was fake.

She primped a strand of her hair behind her ear before she noticed me at the door. With caution, she closed her lipstick and smiled.

"Uh . . . are you going somewhere, Mom?" I questioned, gripping my fingers against the featureless, porcelain door frame.

"Yes, I am," she answered, dropping her lipstick into a rose pink, striped make-up bag. "I'm going out to dinner with a couple of friends."

"When will you be back?" I asked, stepping one foot on the tiled floor of the bathroom.

"I should be back by eight or nine," Mom replied, tossing her beige Michael Kors handbag on her shoulder. "I won't stay out too long. It'll only be a couple of hours, Rylie."

I nodded my head as she turned back to the mirror. She took out a make-up compact from her bag and started to do a few touch ups to her forehead. Within a minute, she closed it gently and placed it back into her purse.

"I'm going to get going now. I'll see you later. Love you," Mom strutted to me, reaching her arms out to me for a hug. Her fingers grasped against my bag tightly, along with her arms. The hug felt tight, like a bear hug.

"I love you, too," I wiggled myself free from the hug to breathe.

"Also, don't forget to take out Cookie's litter and wash the dishes," she ordered with a calm expression.

"I won't," I groaned.

"Good," she said, reaching into her handbag to retrieve her phone. She sauntered out of the bathroom and bedroom to walk out into the hall. I followed her and watched her climb down the stairs. I trailed behind her to observe her strut out of the door, heading for the kitchen afterwards.

I squinted my eyes for a moment, the tip of my finger planted on my chin. Normally, my mother almost never went out to dinner with friends. Sure, sometimes she hung out with them, but not to the point where they would stay out for dinner. Maybe she's trying something new. I mean, she's been working a lot just to provide. She deserves a break after all, so I'll give it to her.

08. Paintings

BY THE END of the school day on September twenty-fourth, the corridors of Crews were filled with posters that promoted the art competition. The bulletin board near the art hallway was a perfect example of this. There were at least two posters that contained all the information about TCVA. I stopped dead in my tracks to take a peek at them.

It's only been a day since the contest has started. I haven't succeeded in finding something I want to paint for it. Since I like to paint buildings, outdoor scenery, and everything related to that, I kind of already have an idea of what things I'm going to paint, but I still don't know exactly what to paint.

According to the posters, the judges want something that reflects off of the real world, whether it would be emotions, actions, or whatever. I have to admit that this is the part that stumped me most. It led me to be even more hesitant on what to paint. Art is my way of expressing how I feel at times, so why can't I figure out what to paint?

"I'll meet you at my house in about twenty-five, buttercup," a familiar, masculine voice hummed from meters behind me.

"That sounds great, Axel. Love you," a feminine voice gleamed.

My head spun around to whoever was behind me. From the sound of their voices, I already knew that it was Axel and his girlfriend, Adrienne. I was correct. The two exchanged a quick kiss before Adrienne sauntered down the broad corridor, heading towards the nearest stairwell. Axel, however, strutted closer to me.

"Looks like you've been looking at all this, Eli," Axel said, glimpsing at the prizes poster that was fastened to the board.

"Yeah," I planted my hands on my hips.

"Have you seen the prizes you can get by winning? They're great," He questioned, interest enchanting in his voice.

"I'll take a look at them," I answered, turning to the poster that contained the prize information.

For the entire day, my mind has been caught up on the contest, not the prizes. My face focused on the poster that listed all of the prizes, scanning every word I could see. The poster listed that the first place winner could win tickets to Italy, an art scholarship to Laurier University, and a one-thousand dollar cash prize.

My mouth dropped open in awe as a pang of determination rushed my veins. The prize is perfect. A vacation to Italy sounds relaxing. I'm dying to try out some Italian food and visit various monuments there. A one-thousand dollar cash prize also sounds great too, considering that I'm basically broke, besides the money I make at work.

What caught my eye most for some reason was the scholarship. Getting the scholarship would be enough to convince my parents that I have potential to become an artist. If I don't win first place in this contest, I don't know what I'll do. I'm already having a difficult time figuring out what I'm going to paint for the contest, and if I don't figure it out, first place may end up being awarded to Axel. The competition is for high school students in our city, so I have many people to compete with, but then again, Axel won TCVA for the past two years.

I need ideas. I need to understand what the judges want for the contest. I need answers. There's only one person I know that could answer them.

I abandoned the bulletin board and made a sharp turn to the art corridor, heading straight to the end to Ms. Edwards' classroom. Before I entered, I peeked my head into the doorframe to make sure the classroom wasn't abandoned. Ms. Edwards was at the sink area of the classroom, organizing paint brushes into buckets while humming a melodious tune to herself.

I felt the bottom of my shoes squeak against the tiled floor as I strutted to where she was. Her head shot up from the package she was looking into and flashed a warm smile to me.

"Hi, Ms. Edwards. May I ask you a question?" I questioned, my hands planted to the table I was in front of.

"Ask away, Mr. Greene," Ms. Edwards gleamed before setting a box on the floor.

"I read the information about TCVA and I'm a bit confused about the contest's theme. The description said that the judges are looking for artwork that reflects off of the real world physically and emotionally," I said. "I don't know what to paint that would match what they want."

Ms. Edwards paused for a minute to process everything I stated and planted her finger on her chin. "Since the judges want artwork that reflects off of the world in that way, think of something that would represent something that expresses an emotion. You'll figure it out."

"Yeah, but the thing is, I don't know what to do. It's like everything I think of isn't right for the contest," I reasoned, glimpsing down at my classic, black and white Vans.

"I see. Since you like scenery, surround yourself around it. Sit somewhere outdoors and ponder about what you're going to do. Feel free to get inspired by other paintings," Ms. Edwards hauled an unopened package from the floor to the countertop. "When you figure it out, you're more than welcome to stay here in my classroom to work on your painting if you wish." Her eyes darted to the door, focusing on Axel who curiously stood there. "Same for you, Axel."

"That sounds great. Thank you, Ms. Edwards," Axel combed a finger through his shaggy, raven hair that covered his olive green eyes.

"Yeah, thank you," I acknowledged before making a zig-zag through the art tables to the door.

The howl of the wind blowing against the leaves of trees and the bristles of grass felt relaxing. I crouched down under a pine tree, gaining a glimpse of the large lake ahead of me. This spot is my relaxation hangout spot. There are no blaring noises of cars on trucks, or the foggy smell of them. There's only the calm sound of birds chirping and the natural scent of the pine trees and grass.

I reached towards my backpack that was tossed on the ground and pulled out my sketchpad, my back leaned on a rough tree trunk of an aged oak tree. My eyelids shut as I breathed in, pondering about what I'll paint for the contest. All I thought about was the woods and that only, which didn't fit the theme for the contest in a way.

I reached for my phone, which was stuffed in my back pocket and pulled out my awfully tangled earbuds, tied up in knots and twists. I plugged in the jack and stuffed them in, my fingers pressed on the Spotify icon that led me to the app. I played a random study music playlist and slouched back. I may not be studying, but it might still help me focus on seeking ideas.

No matter how much time I brainstormed, nothing came to mind. Nothing that would be suitable for the contest, at least.

"Clouds . . . too plain. Skyscrapers . . . that won't match the contest's theme," I mused before groaning at a random advertisement that blasted through my earbuds. "Drats."

I tossed my backpack on my shoulder and stood up, my feet brushed against the pine tree leaves scattered against the ground. I sauntered towards the wooden dock of the lake, plopping myself at the rim, my fingers planted against it. The rush of the water was soothing. This place was a location where people could fish and hang out, but fewer people started to come, so it became a quiet place where hardly anyone went to. At least, I never saw anyone stop by here.

But I guess I said that too soon.

"Hey," a voice mused from a distance. "Do you mind me staying here for a bit?"

09. Their Place

RYLIE

THE LAKE IN town was yet another location I enjoyed hanging out at whenever I wanted peace and quiet. The soothing sound of the leaves on trees swaying and the rush of the lake was my solace. It was occasional for me to come by the lake and stay there, since I didn't want to bump into people—if people came by this lake anyway. I stand corrected.

When I reached the dock a minute ago, Elias was the first thing I saw, his hands rubbing his temples. I didn't expect him to come by the lake, that's for sure. Everything has been quiet since I arrived here, but that's fine. I didn't come here to chat. I came here to relax a bit before I head home. Elias, however, had an opened sketchpad in his hands, along with a pencil. From my view, there wasn't a single pencil mark in sight. Maybe I wasn't seeing things well because I was distanced from him, but I didn't bother to lean in closer. It wasn't my business, anyway.

He reached for his phone, which was stuffed into his back pocket, connected to his tangled earbuds. I grimaced at all the knots I saw in them. They looked just as tangled as mine, but probably not in a worse case. Seriously, earbuds should be made in a way where the wires won't tangle that much. There's already a solution—wireless earbuds—but I feel like they'd get lost much easier.

The mumble of swear words disrupted my thoughts. My head shot up to Elias, who was gliding his pencil across his paper, gawking at his paper.

"W-What are you doing?" I couldn't help but question from curiosity, my eyes widened.

"I'm thinking of something to paint for an art contest, Crews City Visual Arts," he replied, his eyes fixated on his sketch pad before he turned to me. "But I still can't figure it out."

"What does your painting have to be about?" I questioned.

"Well, I know that it has to reflect the world, and I get that, but the judges are looking for something that reflects off the world emotionally. I just don't know what to do," he answered, his fingers brushing against the aged mahogany wood of the dock.

I placed a finger at the tip of my chin. It'll be a piece of cake to think of an idea, considering what I experience every day. What I feel outside is different from what I feel outside, mainly because I hide it from others. My internal emotions don't match my outer emotions, and it's never been okay. It'll never be.

"What if you paint a person . . . A person who feels different from how they feel outside than how they feel on the inside. They can feel cheerful on the outside, but different internally. That's your choice, though," I suggested out of the blue.

Elias' finger brushed against his chin, his eyes lit up, like the sunrise in a clear sky. "Wow . . . you're such a genius. I totally didn't even think of that. Thank you so much, Rylie!" He gleamed. "That's your name, right?"

"Yeah, it is," I chuckled. "And what can I say except you're welcome?"

A roar of laughter escaped his mouth, his hands gripping against the edges of his sketchpad. "I'm going to find a way to thank you a lot more than this. This contest means a lot to me," his eyes twinkled, like a glimmering star.

"Just saying thank you was enough. There's no need to go beyond that," I insisted, startled from the vibration of my phone.

I rummaged it out of the back pocket of my jeans and powered it on. The first thing that popped up was a text message from Nora. I tapped it, only to reveal the full message.

Nora, 4:16 PM:Ry, where are you? I thought that we were gonna meet at your house today but you aren't here.

Me, 4:17 PM: Oh right. I forgot all about that. I'll be home in about ten minutes. Hang on.

Nora, 4:17 PM:Sounds like a plan. See you in ten!

"I gotta go. See you later," I rose up from the dock, the wood of it creaking like an old door.

"Bye," he turned to me for a second before staring back at his sketch pad.

As soon as my foot stepped on the lush, juniper green grass, I picked up my feet and ran as if I was on fire. It would take me a good five minutes to get home at this rate. I completely forgot that Nora and I were supposed to hang out after school today. Maybe because it was a last-minute plan. That's probably why it just bounced off of my brain.

By the time I reached the exit that led to the lake, which was basically a dirt path with pine leaves, twigs, grass bristles, and miniature rocks scattered all over it. It wasn't anything special, but it led to somewhere where I could hang out in peace. I first discovered this place when my mother and father divorced. Whenever I wasn't isolated in my room—which was rare—I came to this place. At first, I thought that it was the woods. But once I got deeper into the land, it wasn't. It was a lake and a large area of grass and trees.

It was quite impressive. It was probably the only highlight of my life at the time of the divorce, and that meant something. Just thinking about the divorce made me shake my head in disbelief. I pinched my arm so I wouldn't get side-tracked. I was about to cross the road, after all. If I crashed into a car, that would be a problem—a severe one. Mom would be upset if I got hurt—which would definitely happen.

The thoughts of my mother being upset disturbed me to the point where I was biting my nails, sweat beading down my forehead.

I could never bear seeing my mother hurt. That will only hurt me more than I already am. A broken heart doesn't need to be broken all over again. The continuous honk of a car horn disrupted my thoughts, causing me to snap back into focus. Looks like I got side-tracked again. Fortunately, my house was already in view. I was right in front of it, too. Nora's Corolla was parked on the driveway. Once I reached the driver's seat, I didn't see her there. She must be inside. It looks like Mom is home, too.

I rummaged my house key from my side pocket, lint stuffed on the sides of it. I brushed it off with my thumb and twisted it through the door knob. The door flung open, allowing me to walk in. I slipped my shoes off and placed them in front of the door, my socks gliding against the caramel, hardwood floor as I sauntered through the foyer and the living room. Nora was seated at the kitchen table, her eyes glued to her phone, while Mom was raiding the fridge.

"I'm home," I announced, a small grin plastered across my face.

"Ry! You're finally here. I've been waiting forever," Nora gleamed, placing her phone face-down on the table as she stood up from her chair, the legs of it screeching as it slid against the tiled floor.

"Yeah, I let her in when she was at the door. Where were you?" Mom questioned, curiosity lightning in her eyes. "When you came home from school three hours ago, you dropped your things off and left all of a sudden."

"I was at the lake. You know, the one I used to hang out at," I replied without a doubt.

"Oh, alright. Anyway, I'm going to go to work for a few hours. I'll be back by seven, Rylie," she reversed the topic, reaching for a beige manila folder that was placed on the countertop. "Feel free to treat yourselves to anything you'd like in the refrigerator. If not, you can order something."

"Okay, see you later, Mom," I nodded my head, sauntering towards the fridge.

The heels of her shoes clicked against the floor, the sounds growing softer until she bolted out. I opened the refrigerator, hoping to find something to eat.

"Do you want anything to eat, Nora?" I offered, glimpsing at her.

"Yeah. I am kind of hungry. What's in the fridge?" She questioned, pushing her chair under the table to approach me.

"A little bit of leftover spaghetti from two days ago, fruits, veggies, orange juice, and salad dressing," I grimaced at the scarcity in front of me.

"Well we can order some food, like a pizza or something," Nora suggested, reaching for her phone on the table, the fake gems in her phone case shimmering like stars in the night sky.

"Good idea. I have some money around here somewhere. I just have to find it in my room," I rushed towards the foyer, climbing onto the stairs with caution.

Nora trailed behind me. I climbed up each step with caution, as if I were climbing a mountain. Once I reached the top, I circled around them to my bedroom, the door open slightly. I opened my first drawer, looking into it. My wallet was in there somewhere. Cookie snuggled against my feet with a purr. I chuckled, reaching for my wallet, which was somehow under a folded, oversized T-shirt

I haven't worn since sophomore year. I raised an eyebrow, baffled on how it got there.

I unzipped the zipper to reveal what was inside. There were a couple of one-dollar bills, four to be exact. Based on what I had, there isn't enough to purchase a pizza.

"I don't have enough money," I grimaced, turning to Nora.

"Luckily, I have some money," she gleamed, gesturing to her credit card from her wallet. "We can put it on my card."

"But don't you need to save up for Kylie's eyeshadow palette?" I questioned, pushing my drawer closed with my hands.

"It'll only be a couple of dollars. Don't worry," she tutted, pulling her phone from her back pocket. "Veggie pizza does sound good, right?"

"Yeah, it does," I answered, slouching down at the rim of my bed. "I'll make sure to pay you back for all this."

"Nah, no need," Nora insisted, dialing a number on her phone.

Once the number was picked up, an employee from the pizza chain greeted her, questioning what we wanted to order. My friend recited our order, adding in an orange Fanta. My stomach growled just thinking about savoring pizza and washing it down with Fanta. It wasn't exactly healthy, but after a long, tiring day, I deserve it.

"Pizza's here!" Nora announced from the doorframe of my room, a pizza box with a liter of Fanta on top of it in hand.

The mouthwatering aroma of the pizza flew out of the holes at the side of the box, invading the room at an instant. I inhaled, ready to ingest a slice. My friend set the box at the center of my bed, and the Fanta on my nightstand, along with a few plastic cups, paper plates, and napkins. I opened the box, revealing the enchanting sight of numerous vegetables, such as tomatoes, onions, and peppers smudged next to each other. I grabbed a paper plate from my nightstand and ripped off a slice, reaching it towards my mouth. The peppery taste melted in my mouth as I consumed my first bite.

"I'm dreading school tomorrow," Nora groaned, pouring herself Fanta into a cup, the surface bubbling. "I have to return that design book I borrowed two weeks ago."

"That sucks. The other day, I went to the school library to borrow a book, but I ended up borrowing the maximum amount," I murmured, disappointment in my eyes.

"Wow, that's sad," she grimaced before taking a bite from her slice.

Reading is a distraction to me—a good one. It diverts me from what's happening around me, which is something I've desperately needed since what happened a few years ago. When I was at the school library the other day, I discovered a couple of books I've never heard of that seemed interesting. Too bad I couldn't check them out.

The noise of Nora pulling something out of her mocha brown miniature backpack disrupted my thoughts, the slams of a couple of her perfume containers smashing together. She pulled out her full-size rose gold iPad, the fake silver gems she plastered on the sides glimmering. She powered it on with her thumb, clicking the Instagram icon that led to her newest post, which was a cute outfit inspiration—ripped jeans, black and white Converse shoes, a porcelain striped crop top with cuts at the edges, and a couple of handmade accessories laid on a fluffy, white surface.

"My latest Instagram post got two-hundred likes," she squealed like a person who seen a newborn baby, zooming in to maximize her post.

"Wow, that is so cool. You only posted that a few hours ago, too," I examined the comments of the post, my eyes skimming through each.

You always have the best outfits, AdrienneGriffin17 commented. This looks so aesthetic. I love it, TotallyNotAyden complimented. The rest of the visible comments went on and on with well-deserved comments. Nora always dreamt of becoming a fashion designer when she becomes older. It makes sense, considering that she turns old, plain clothes into something new. While me, on the other hand, still can't decide on what to become.

Any jobs that involve the human brain sounds interesting, so maybe I could be something related to psychology. I don't know what in particular though, but I'll figure it out one day. Before I graduate, at least.

?

10. Suck It Up (Take One)

ELIAS

THE SCHOOL'S PERFORMING Arts Center was usually peaceful during lunch hour, like a field of daisies. Only a few students vacated the area, mainly the auditorium. Normally, only theatre kids hang out here around this time, and a couple of other students. Sometimes, Cannon and I hang out around here often when the lunchroom is too animated for our liking. My top reason for adoring to hang out here is that I have all of lunch period to finish up missing homework.

Lunch period lasts around forty minutes, half for lunchtime and the other half for study hall in the Commons—or anywhere, really.

Today, I plan on spending it to start rough-sketching my painting for the art contest. Thanks to Rylie, I know what I'm going to paint. I'll paint a person with various emotions inside and out or something like that. I found it impressive that she thought of something pretty quickly without pausing for a couple of minutes to think about it.

I pulled out my sketch pad from my backpack, turning to a clean page as my fingers brushed against the rough cover. I pulled my juniper green mechanical pencil from the anchor grey binding. I brushed the pencil across my paper to form an oval. It wasn't the best, but it wasn't the worst. It didn't matter because I was only drawing a rough sketch.

"You've already started on your sketch?" Cannon questioned, observing my sketchpad closely.

"Yeah," I nodded. "I think I'll work on this until lunch period is over."

"Lucky. I have to finish my homework for marketing," he groaned, gesturing to his ruby red two-inch binder, a folded paper sprawled its surface.

"Good luck with that," I grimaced, reaching towards the floor. I pulled my frigid water bottle, water cascading my fingers. I cracked it open and placed it on my mouth, the bottle making a glug sound. Sketching may be my getaway, but it can be tiring. I formed two lines with my pencil for a neck, and two arch-ish lines to connect to those, alongside the head to form a body. My pencil circled around the top area of the head to form curly hair. It wasn't perfect, but it will be improved once this is painted on a canvas.

I divided the person in half with a sturdy line down the middle. Before I could start sketching details, an animated, feminine laugh of someone interrupted me. The chuckle grew louder until it approached the row Cannon and I were sitting on. It was two of our classmates, Rylie and her friend. I think Nora is her name.

"Let's sit here," she proclaimed to Rylie, who shrugged. "Cannon and his friend are here so we won't have to be alone."

"Hi," Cannon and I gleamed in sync. He gestured to the empty seat to his right for Nora to sit on with a welcoming grin before they started chatting about the usual—fashion and design. Rylie plopped herself on the idle seat to my right, the fresh aroma of lavender laundry detergent from her sweater prickling my nose. She powered on her phone, her eyes fixated on her home screen.

"Hey," I said vaguely, causing her head to shoot up from her phone. "I just wanted to thank you once again for everything. I've started on my rough sketch and this means so much to me."

"Again, you're welcome," she shrugged, placing her phone face-down on her lap. "I'm just wondering... why does it mean so much to you? Is it because you want to become an artist in the future?"

"Well, yeah. I figured this contest would give me an extra boost," I explained before taking a sip of my water. "Long story short, my parents don't think I should become an artist in the future, so I need to do everything I can to convince them that I can be one. They think that I won't make enough money to be an artist if that's my only job."

"Seriously?" Rylie raised an eyebrow. "I mean, if you become interested in selling your artwork, you'd make a lot. You'd probably need an extra job to be on the safe side, but I think this is a good opportunity for you. You're great at creating art."

"You have a point. Thanks," I nodded, tucking my water bottle into the side pocket of my backpack, the plastic making a crack noise.

She hummed in response before she turned back to her phone, her finger running down the screen. I turned to Cannon, who was deep in conversation with Nora, like two children who hadn't seen each other in days. They were viewing various Pinterest posts on their phones, each of them having practically one hue in each.

"Elias," he turned to me, gesturing to Nora's phone. "Aren't these aesthetics so cute? The cyan one is my favorite."

"They are," I nodded.

"I made them myself, so thanks," Nora squealed like a person looking at a newborn baby, reaching down towards the floor for her backpack. "Also, does anyone want mini doughnuts? I got them this morning before school and didn't eat them all."

"I'll have some. I haven't eaten since breakfast, so thank you" I gestured to my rumbling stomach. She hummed, passing the bag to me. I unfolded the bag to reveal the miniature doughnuts with sprinkles plastered on top with various hues, the taffy pink icing dripping on the sides. There were three of them in the bag, overlapping each other. "Do you want one, Cannon?" I questioned, snatching his attention away from his phone.

"Yes, thank you, Eli," he gleamed, extending his hand inside the bag to grab one.

"No prob," I muttered, my head shooting to my right. Rylie sat there quietly, her eyes now dug into a book, earbuds jammed in her ears. She's been silent for the entire time. No words came out of her mouth, not even a peep. I wasn't shocked, considering she was always this way, at least in art class she was. She hardly spoke, and when she did, it was always with her friend.

She seems to concentrate a lot on what she does. I pretty much do the same whenever I'm working on something art-related, but otherwise, not really. I'm not loud, but I'm not quiet either. I guess you can say that I'm in the middle of the scale.

I dug my hand into the bag and grabbed a doughnut, the icing painted on my fingers. When I took a bite, the savory taste of thick jelly filling melted in my mouth, along with the sprinkles. Jelly doughnuts have always been my personal favorite. I'd have them over any other doughnut, and I mean any. Now, there was only one doughnut remaining in the bag. It would be fair to ask Rylie if she wanted it, especially since Nora asked if anyone wanted them and she probably didn't hear.

"Uh, Rylie, do you want a doughnut? They're jelly, by the way," I offered her, widening the top of the bag to show her what was inside.

"Sure, and thank you," she extended her hand inside the bag, the front area of her mocha natural curls shadowing her eyes.

"Mhm," I balled the bag to form a paper ball.

I pulled out a napkin from my pocket, wiping the icing off my hands. I crumbled it before grasping it against the so-called paper bag, rising up from my chair. "Excuse me," I muttered, gesturing to Rylie's feet that didn't allow me to move. She moved her feet under her seat and I made my departure to a nearby trash can near the main exit door of the auditorium. I successfully tossed my trash in without a miss, turning towards where I was seated after. When I got to my seat, the noise of the bell blared.

I groaned while my hand ran up the right strap of my backpack. I didn't want lunch to end, especially since I hadn't gotten far in sketching. I can always finish it at home, or even further into the school day if I have time. I shoved my sketchbook into my backpack, lifted it up from the floor, and tossed the straps on my shoulders.

"I don't want to go to English," Cannon complained as he stretched. "I'll see you all in art."

"Yeah. Let's go, Ry. See you all later," Nora said, her hand placed on Rylie's shoulder.

The three made their departure out of the auditorium, me trailed behind them. The performing arts wing wasn't too crowded, so I abandoned the wing quickly. I made a sharp turn towards the stairwell, my eyes focused on a familiar boy who was slowly walking through the halfway surface of the stairs, his phone in hand. Obviously, it was Axel based on the shaggy black outfit and an outfit that consisted of only grey, black, and white. I caught up to him, causing his attention to shoot up from his phone.

"Hi, Axel," I muttered casually.

"Hey, Eli," he proclaimed, his eyes lightening up. "Have you thought about anything to paint for TCVA yet? I have."

"I actually have, and I even started sketching it out today," I replied without a doubt.

"That's nice. I'm going to start mine soon," he announced, a hand running through his raven black hair. "You're up for a competition, Elias."

"I already knew that, but thanks for the reminder," I gleamed, my grin quickly fading into a grimace.

"It's just a reminder," the brunet shrugged his shoulders as the five-minute warning bell rang. As soon as he reached the top of the steps, he disappeared to the right of the corridor within a trace. I groaned, rubbing my temples. Considering the way Axel acts, I wasn't surprised. I've known Axel for just as long as I've known Cannon, which was since about kindergarten. We were never friends or enemies. We were in between, I guess.

Whenever we had art projects or anything that involved drawing or painting, there was always a competition between him and I, like who would get a better grade on their assignment. We used to challenge each other to see who would get a golden star and who wouldn't. Half of the time, it was me. The other half was him. This continued throughout the rest of elementary and middle school, as well as now. The only thing that changed is that it wasn't so childish anymore. There were no more golden star stickers or drawing random objects.

Everything became advanced and challenging, and it'll stay that way.

11. Hardwork

RYLIE

BEFORE TODAY, I never saw an angry customer in action before my eyes. Sure, I've seen angry customers on videos—or at least heard of them—but in the end, I haven't seen one personally. Today is a normal Sunday, right before dinnertime, too. I decided to stop by Taco Fiesta to purchase tacos for Mom and I to take home. The angry woman who was in front of me in line yelled at the staff, all while holding to her daughter's hand, who seemed like she wanted to wander off because she constantly pulled on her mother's jacket sleeve with her other hand.

"Mommy," the child whined, yanking her hand away from hers. "I'm hungry! I want to eat now."

"Stay quiet, honey. You wouldn't still be hungry if certain people would get your order ready faster,," the woman snarled to the boy who was located at the cash register, who looked like he was about to snap at the lady, but gulped down the urge.

"Ma'am, I'm sorry about all this. Your order will be finished soon," he insisted in a calm manner, peeking back at the kitchen area. He grabbed a small, kid-sized cup from below the counter, dashing towards the drink fountain afterwards. He filled the cup with ice and a ruby red drink that seemed to be fruit punch. The nozzle made a whirring noise after the cup was full as the employee attached a cap to the drink, grabbing an individually packaged straw. He slid the drink across the counter, handing it to the little girl who mumbled a satisfied "thank you" to him.

I guess I haven't paid attention to his features or to his voice because he was oddly familiar. From under the raven black hat he was wearing, I could see dark brown naturally curly hair in the back as he turned to adjust something. It was Elias, obviously. I was a bit surprised that he works here, and even more surprised that he managed to deal with an angry customer so peacefully. He didn't snap or walk away to get one of his co-workers to deal with the lady. He remained calm, which I have to admit is something that I probably wouldn't do if that were my job.

When the woman's order was finally ready, Elias gently handed it to her, which her daughter took from her. The woman scoffed and held her daughter's hand, sauntering off to the nearest table. I stepped forward, my hands gripped against the hard surface of the counter.

"Hi, Rylie. I didn't expect to see you here," he sighed with relief. "I'm sorry I didn't take your order beforehand, but what can I get for you?"

"Hey, it's okay. I'm not in much of a rush, anyway," I insisted, my head shot up to the large menu overhead. "I'd like to have a mixed taco and nacho combo with two cinnamon rolls, please."

"Alright, do you want any drinks?" He questioned while typing everything into the register.

"Yes, may I have two small Sprites?" I requested in sync.

"Sure thing. Your total will be twenty-four ninety-five. Cash, credit, or debit?"

"Cash," I said, reaching into the pocket of my hoodie. I fished out a twenty dollar bill, as well as a five dollar bill. I handed it to him and he placed it into the register, cupping a few coins into his hand for change. He dropped it into my hand and I placed it in my pocket.

"Your order will be ready in a few minutes," he announced as he pulled out two cups from under the counter. He inserted ice into both cups and put both cups under the Sprite nozzle on the drinking fountain. A series of disruptive whirring blasted after he finished using the machine. After the caps were placed on the cups, he pulled a cup holder from the end of the counter and placed both cups on them, the straws in the middle.

"It must've been a lot to deal with customers l-like . . . those," I whispered, gesturing to the lady who made a scene earlier.

"Tell me about it," Elias rolled his eyes. "I had to resist every urge to not snap at her."

"You did a great job remaining calm, you know. If I were you at that time, I would've snapped right away, to be honest," I admitted, a dry laugh escaping my mouth.

"Thanks, and I tried my best not to," he chuckled, adjusting his hat. An employee placed my order on the counter behind him with a whistle. He gently held the handle of the thin, colorful cardboard box and handed it to me.

"Thank you," I lifted the cup holder with one hand, the fingers of my other hand grasped to the box. "I have to get going now. My mother is waiting for me outside and I think I've taken long enough. I'll see you tomorrow, Elias."

"Bye," a broad smile spread across his face.

I mustered a smile and sauntered past the tables that led to the exit. When I reached outside, the aroma of food cooking and traditional music playing came to a halt. Now, the only thing I smelled and heard was gas and the blare of car horns, as well as the engine of Mom's car running. Her car was parked directly outside the restaurant, so I entered, placing the cup holder on the floor before I got seated.

"What took you so long, Rylie?" She questioned curiously, putting down her phone to place it in her handbag.

"It was busy inside," I stated briefly as I fastened my seatbelt.

"Oh, alright," she nodded, tying her mocha brown wavy hair into a ponytail before setting the car wheels on reverse.

I purposely left out the part where I was speaking with Elias, mainly because of the reaction she could've had. She wouldn't be mad or anything—she would just get too excited because I was "finally speaking with someone new for once," as she would say. My best friend, Nora, was practically the only person I've spoken with that wasn't family for the past few years. Mom always encouraged me to make new friends and talk to people more often, but that alone isn't the easiest thing. It's never been, and it probably never will be. Maybe I've made a little bit of progress, but those are just . . . baby steps.

The rest of the car ride home was silent. The only thing that could be heard was the whirring of the air conditioner. It's the season of fall, but it's quite hot outside, specifically in the afternoon. The sun was shining way too bright for my liking. I'll always prefer cloudy days—or better yet—rainy days, and it's already clear why. Rainy days just feel more . . . comfortable.

Once we got home, I immediately took the food to the kitchen table after taking off my shoes. Mom always hated when shoes were worn in the house. She always complained of how unsanitary and gross it was to take germs from outside to take them inside. I couldn't blame her, to be honest. It's more comfortable to not wear shoes—unless their cozy bed slippers in the house.

I opened the box to reveal the mouthwatering food inside. Everything was either wrapped in paper or packaged in a disposable container. I set everything on the table, as well as the drinks while Mom placed two plates for both of us on the table. When everything was done, we both sat down and dug in. The zesty smell of the tacos prickled my nose, as well as the spicy aroma of guacamole and salsa in the nacho plates. Mexican food was a food that I've always adored, especially when I was younger.

I remember when my father and I went on picnics and we ordered tacos, tortillas, nachos, and just about anything else you could think of. My eyes watered a bit, not in a distressed way, but in a gleeful way. Although it triggered certain memories, it was beautiful to experience at the time.

"So, how was your day?" Mom questioned after opening the lid for the salsa.

"It was fine, I guess, yours?" I replied in sync, unwrapping a hard-shelled taco from its wrapping.

"Mine was okay, but work has been tiring. I couldn't even cook dinner for us tonight," she sighed, rubbing her eye temples with her fingers.

For the past few years, Mom had to work twice as much as she used to. Being a single mother had a heavy toll on her. Keeping a roof over our heads, paying dozens of bills, providing food for us, and just about everything else meant she had to work continuously, about twice as much as she worked before.

It would've been partially reasonable for her to take some kind of break, but would that be possible? No matter what, there is some money that'll need to be stored just in case something happens. But what exactly are the possibilities of something happening? At the end of the day, they bills have to paid and food has to be put on the table. It's unknown what unexpected event will happen at any time.

12. Loosen Up

ELIAS

BY THE FOLLOWING week, the broad corridors of the school were filled with red and white decorations for the start of homecoming week. The cheerleading squad marched throughout the halls, the bows stuck in their hair glistened through the artificial light. Homecoming week was filled with various activities, like pep rallies and dances. I've never participated much in homecoming week, including the dances.

I've never had anyone to go to the dance with, other than just friends. I'm completely okay with it because school dances were never my thing. They've never caught my eye, anyway. Well, except for the dozens of glittery posters plastered on the plain porcelain brick walls.

"Rylie, look at this," I heard Nora gleam from a distance away, her hand nudging Rylie's arm. "The homecoming dance is on Friday. We should definitely check it out. It'll be so much fun!"

"No way. I don't like school dances at all. There's too many people there and all that jazz," Rylie persisted, her hand clutching the sleeves of her golden yellow sweater.

"Aww, that's fine. We don't have to go," Nora hid her disappointment through a smile before turning towards the direction of Cannon and I. "Hey, guys. Are you heading to the pep rally?"

"Yeah," Cannon answered blandly. "Even if it's gonna be kind of lame, it's better than being in class, I guess."

The main gym was just around the corner, so we filed behind dozens of other people heading in that direction. Roars and cheers were said among themselves as everyone piled through the doors that swung open and closed every second. The bleachers were already almost full, a few spaces vacant here and there. Because it would take forever to get to one of the top rows due to everyone getting situated, we settled towards one of the bottom rows towards the middle.

Principal Herrington gently removed a microphone from a stand towards the center of the gym, the microphone making a deafening screeching noise. It caught a lot of people's attention since a majority of people were lost into their phones, deep in conversation, or somehow multitasking between both.

"Good morning, Eagles," the principal announced. "Welcome to today's pep rally and the start of homecoming week!"

A chorus of cheers and claps immediately started, lasting a good moment. Afterwards, Principal Herrington began to explain what would take place today. According to her, there will be a promotion for the school's football team, as well as the cheerleaders. There will also be a basketball game where anyone can participate after that.

"So, does anyone have any plans for homecoming week?" Cannon questioned curiously, a glimmer appearing in his eyes.

"Not really," Rylie and I somehow stated in sync.

"Yeah, same. I'm not going to the dance this year, but we could hang out sometime this week or something," Nora suggested, her fingers brushing on her sleek raven hair which was let down.

"We can hang out at my house today a few hours after school. I can order food and everything," Cannon offered.

"Sounds good," everyone but Rylie nodded.

"You don't want to come, Ry? It'll be fun," Nora insisted, her hand running through her friend's shoulders to massage them. "Please?"

The brunette paused, letting out one big sigh after. "Fine, I'll be there, I guess."

As soon as Cannon mentioned his house, my mind flashed to the several times I've gotten lost in there. He lives in a literal mansion with plenty of land surrounding it. I remember several occasions where I've gotten lost while finding the restroom—and that was just when I was little. His mother was nice enough to show me where it was and it turned out to be around the corner.

It occasionally happens to this day, even if they still live in that same house. I only know one way in and one way out, really. Well, kind of. On the other hand, hanging out sounds good. I don't have much plans for Friday evening other than chilling. Since I wasn't doing anything, I bent down to where my backpack was and pulled out my sketchpad, flipping to the page with the sketch of my entry for the art contest.

Before I knew it, I was making good progress by starting on minor details.

The evening couldn't come soon enough. Before I knew it, Nora, Rylie, and I stood in front of the towering front doors of Cannon's house. The school day actually went by rapidly, probably thanks to the pep rally. The howling wind and the swaying of the leaves that hadn't fallen from the trees yet invaded the area, other than flocks of birds in the sky leaving for migration below the clouds that blanketed the sky.

From inside the house, I heard the door unlock from the inside, meaning someone was at the door. When the door burst open, a woman who had her hazel brown hair in a ponytail and a golden yellow dress with jewelry to match was at the door. It was Cannon's mother, Ms. Daniels.

"Good afternoon, everyone. Please come in," she smiled, stepping out of the doorway to allow us to go in. "Elias, are these your friends? Ayden was expecting you all here."

I introduced them to her as they extended their hands to reach hers for separate hand shakes. They were brief, yet friendly.

"You can just call me Kari," Ms. Daniels gleamed. "Ayden should be downstairs in the basement hangout room on the west wing. Elias can show you where it is. If you need anything, let me know."

We nodded in approval. I gestured Nora and Rylie to the right of the arched, wooden stairway ahead of us, which led to a corridor. We passed through the living room that smelled like vanilla air freshener. There were two champagne-colored sofas and a couple of accent chairs to match. Instead of having porcelain marbled floors like the vast foyer, the floor was carpeted. A frame that contained Cannon's family was fastened to the off-white wall above the expensive-looking fireplace.

When we reached the kitchen, Nora and Rylie's eyes glimmered in shock of how clean it was. Everything looked spotless from our view. There were no stains or dents. It looked as if it's been ripped out of a home design magazine.

"Has anyone ever cooked in this kitchen? It looks so clean," Nora wondered out loud.

"I've always wondered that, too. It's interesting," I pondered as my fingers grasped on the handle of the basement door. We climbed down each step carefully as the artificial light from above guided us down. When I reached the surface, the first thing I saw was Cannon organizing water bottles on the countertop of the hangout room.

The room was pretty clean as well. The sky blue color of the walls highlighted the peach, tiled floor. A random TV show was playing on the flat screen television fastened to the wall, meters in front of a plush mocha brown couch. There were two doors in the room, one that led to a hallway and another that led to outside. Cannon looked up from the countertop with a genuine smile.

"Hey, everyone," he gleamed, extending his hand to shake mine. "I'm so glad you're here. I already ordered food and it's starting to get cold."

"Hi, thanks again for inviting us," Nora stated before she took a seat at one of the chairs at a countertop.

"Yeah, thanks," Rylie muttered as she joined her friend.

"Yeah, thank you, bro," I nodded my head in agreement, peering at the food placed on the lower countertop. It was practically a miniature kitchen in there. "So we have pizza, miniature burgers, water and Sprite. This is going to be great."

"I know, right? Let's start eating," Cannon handed a paper plate to each of us. After that, he rolled up the bulky, juniper green sleeves of his hoodie and opened both of the pizza boxes he ordered, as well as the packaging for the burgers. We all crowded around the area, picking up whichever food we desired to ingest. I ended up having two slices of pepperoni pizza on my plate and a mini burger so far. I sat at one of the chairs in front of the counter, which left one more for Cannon.

"Do any of you all have plans for Halloween?" I questioned out of curiosity, my eyes lightening.

"Not really, I might just stay here in chill," Cannon replied.

Nowadays, people hangout and host and attend parties, whether if it's a seasonal party or just . . . a party. It is no surprise, it's just that parties were never my thing. Really, I've never been to an actual party before, besides parties hosted by family members. I just don't know what to do when it comes to parties. I prefer chill hangouts. Not anything extra, but something normal. Today is a prime example of that. I'm surrounded with people I know with food that's quite normal. Nothing fancy. Just normal.

I'm a pretty plain person, so there isn't anything else to expect from me. There isn't anything special or unusual. I'm just a basic high school student who aspires to become an artist. There's nothing out of the ordinary about that, really. I'm just an average student.

13. Suck It Up (Take Two)

RYLIE

BY THE TIME I got home, I slouched down on the couch next to my mother watching some reality show on TV, her laptop in her lap as she typed into it. She seemed pleased that I hung out with friends for an hour or so, considering that it's pretty unlikely for me to do so. The thing is, I don't know if I can call Elias and Cannon a friend to me just yet. We've only talked on certain occasions. Not about anything personal or anything, but just normal things. They're sweet just like Nora.

"So, did you have fun? You seemed to have made more friends," she smiled as she turned away from the blinding screen of her laptop.

"I guess," I shrugged nonchalantly. "It's not a big deal."

"To you it's not, but I'm glad you're at least stepping out of your comfort zone a little," she reasoned, picking up a glass of wine from the accent table in front of her to take a sip. "Who are your new friends?"

"Right now, they're just people I met when school started. Their names are Elias and Cannon. These two, Nora, and I hung out today. It was chill," I said nonchalantly. "It wasn't anything serious."

"That's nice to hear," she rubbed my shoulder with her hand. "Just remember if things escalate, there's no boys allowed in my house. Particularly upstairs."

"I know, I know," I nagged, my voice slurred.

It's not like I'd have a valid reason to invite a boy into the house and take them up to my bedroom for certain reasons. Not for anything inappropriate, but for anything, really. Getting a boyfriend is just beyond my level at this point. It's not that I'm not interested—I am. It's just that I can hardly make moves that'll get me one. I can hardly even get through the lunch line at school without being asked to speak up while placing my order.

The point is, I'm a quiet person. Love doesn't come to you. You have to find it, and to do that, you have to make some type of move. That means building up a stable friendship that has potential to turn into something more than that. Making friends isn't quite the easiest thing, especially for me since it involves lots of interacting. Getting a boyfriend wouldn't be any easier. But that's fine, I guess. I'm not interested in anyone like that just yet.

I want to hear some stories about how people get a significant other. Not through a book or anything, but something in real life. Come to think of it, I've never actually asked Mom specifically how she managed to date Dad. I've asked how she met him, but there might be more to the story. I just know the basics.

"Mom . . ." I whispered out of curiosity, my eyes lightening up. "I've been wondering . . . at what age did you start dating Dad? And how did you manage to get him to be your boyfriend at the time?"

"Well," she kept a straight face, gently placing her now empty wine glass on the accent table to place her finger on her chin. "We started dating when we were about seventeen. We were really close friends beforehand, so that's how it all began. Obviously, it lasted a while but it eventually came to an end. I had to stay strong through it all."

"I can tell," I mused.

"At the end of the day, I got through everything. I'm thirty-six now. Yes, my relationship with your father was fun while it lasted, especially towards the beginning. Overall, my point is in order to have a significant other, you have to have a stable relationship with them first," she explained. "From my experience, communication is always key."

I paused for a second, thinking over everything that was recently stated. She had a point. Communication is key in a relationship, romantic or not. It prevents misunderstandings and confusion. It makes everything seem closer. It's key. Of course, that wouldn't be the easiest thing for me to get adjusted to.

Heck, I can't even get adjusted to it now. Sure, I'll talk, but only when it's necessary. Maybe I've improved just a bit by talking to people I'm not adapted to fully, namely Cannon and Elias, but I haven't exactly talked to them personally. I never bothered to start an actual conversation with them. Not even alone, to make matters worse. So that isn't much of an improvement.

One step forward, two steps back.

The next morning before school, I found myself in my mother's car, swirling a plastic spoon through baby pink strawberry yogurt. The ride was quiet and all I could think about was how much I just didn't want to come to school. I was in a rush getting ready, so I forgot to get lunch money and my account is nearly empty. With the money that I have, I'll only be able to get a bag of chips.

With the little amount of yogurt I've eaten so far, I won't make it past a period or two before lunch. The default ringtone of my mother's phone sounded throughout the car speakers, ringing my ears. I saw an unfamiliar name on the screen. It was Kaden Casteen. The name flashed on her phone screen, as well. I don't think I know anyone named Kaden, or anyone with the last name Casteen. Whoever was calling Mom is a stranger . . . to me, anyway.

She looked away from the road for a quick second, instantly cracking a smile at the screen. She pressed the traffic light green answer button to make the call hands-free.

"Good morning, Madeline," the guy over the phone chirped.

"Morning, Kaden," she replied before we pulled up at the school's back entrance. "I'll call you back when I reach the office building. I'm dropping off my daughter at school right now. I'll see you there."

"Alright, I'll be here in the main area," Kaden stated before he hung up.

I raised an eyebrow. "Who was that? Who's Kaden, Mom?"

"Kaden is my co-worker," she stated before she pulled up in front of the curb. "Anyway, have a great day at school, Rylie. I'll see you later."

"Bye," I announced as I picked up my backpack from the floor, partially satisfied with the answer she gave me. They seemed awfully close as co-workers, but it's possible, I guess. I tossed it on my shoulder gently before I exited the car. Before I could do that, Mom pulled me in for a tight hug. I wiggled myself free a few moments after and abandoned the car.

Students flooded the entrance, going through all the doors in a not-so-orderly way. I made a zig zag through everyone cautiously, up until I spotted Nora. Her raven hair was wrapped into a high bun. She wore a scarlet cami dress and a white sweater underneath it. She had a bracelet around her wrist to go along with her outfit. As usual, she looks so pretty. Not much in a trendy way, but in a way that she likes.

"Morning, Nora," I chirped as I joined her. "I love your outfit, especially the dress."

"Good morning, Ry," she replied as we entered the building. "Thank you, I got the dress from somewhere in the mall. It would look great on you."

"Dresses really aren't what I like to wear," I rolled my eyes playfully as I reflected off of what was in my closet. I don't have many dresses or skirts in my closet. Come to think of it, I only have one or two that actually fit me. Mom bought them for me not too long ago, but I didn't bother to wear them. They're sundresses, anyway, so it wouldn't make too much sense to wear it now since it's autumn. The clothing I have inside my closet is pretty basic. I just have hoodies, sweaters, T-shirts, and anything else that's considered basic. It suits me just right, I guess. I'm pretty basic, nothing more and probably nothing less.

"Seriously, we should go shopping at the mall sometime. We could get you cute outfits and they would go so well with some of the accessories I made. Trust me," Nora gleamed as if she just saw heaven.

"Maybe, but I will not be buying any dresses or anything that's too pink for that matter," I nudged her arm with a laugh.

"That's reasonable," she nodded as we reached the top of a stairwell.

After a few long hours of my brain being tortured, lunch time approached and we were about halfway through it. I found myself with Nora, Cannon, and Elias at a circular table near a few trash cans in the lunchroom. It wasn't quite the best place to be seated around here, but at least we found somewhere. Instead of us eating school food, Cannon went out of his way to order tacos for us using Uber Eats before lunch even started.

I was questioning how Cannon even managed to get the food from the main office just in time before one of the office ladies threw it away or something, considering around here, students aren't allowed to order food during school hours.

"It was a very close call, but the woman in the office let it slide, thankfully," Cannon winked as he poked a straw into his cup.

"I can tell," Elias grimaced. "But thanks for ordering all this food for us."

"My treat," he gleamed.

After that, it was silent. The lunchroom was still roaring and wild, as usual, but our table grew quiet. I was once the one to start a conversation quite easily, but not anymore. I never know what to talk about. I don't want to start a conversation about anything tedious. Boring people is just something I don't want to do. Maybe I overthink things sometimes, but my point still stands.

"Lately, I've been designing and making scrunchies and accessories and I need some suggestions of what material and color I should use to make my next scrunchie," Nora muttered after she took a bite almost finished taco, the toppings falling into a napkin she spread out on the table. "I've been deciding between satin silver, plaid red, striped blue, or glittery yellow. What should I go with?"

Of course, Nora saved the day.

"I'd go with the plaid red," Elias suggested.

"They all sound nice, I guess, but I think the silver would look nice," I proposed.

"It's between those two and the glittery yellow, but I think I'll need to see them in front of me. Do you have any samples of the materials?" Cannon proposed as he dabbed his lips with a napkin.

"I have all of them laying around in my locker. I can show you them now, if you want," Nora proclaimed, gathering her trash to put it all into a plastic bag.

Cannon nodded in agreement as he gathered his trash to dispose of it in the trash bin inches away from us. After they were finished, they got up from their chairs, walked side-by-side to the exit doors, and disappeared within a trace. Elias and I were left alone, our food still in front of us. It was . . . awkward. Neither of us said anything, not even a peep.

I had a feeling that the remainder of lunch break may stay like this, so I had the unusual urge to start a conversation about something. It'll be distracting, at least.

"So . . ." I muttered. "How is your painting for the art contest you entered?"

"It's been going great. I haven't started painting yet, but my sketch for it is finished," he reasoned.

"That's ... great to hear," I mustered a smile.

He smiled back. "Yeah. This is probably, like, the millionth time I've said this, but thanks again. This all wouldn't have been possible without you, Rylie."

"It's nothing. Nothing at all," I felt my face warm up from all the smiling. "I'm just glad you have something for the contest. Hopefully, you'll win. It's a school contest, right?"

"Well, it's actually a city contest available to students in our school district," he described briefly.

I nodded understandingly before taking a swig of lemonade from my cup. It was nearly finished, so I consumed the entire thing. I was practically finished with my food, so I gathered my trash. Elias was finished as well, so he offered to get up and throw our trash away. I agreed and stayed at the table, pondering on what would happen next. I pulled my phone from my back pocket and turned it on. There was still a good ten minutes of lunch period left.

Elias took a seat in his chair directly across from me. "So ... Are you always like this?"

"Always like what?" I raised an eyebrow.

"Always quiet," he clarified, his hand combing through his curly hair.

"For the past few years, I've been like this, but when I was younger, I was chatty, I guess," I replied honestly. "If you're wondering why, my parents divorced a few years ago. That made me not want to talk anymore, but the death of my Dad just preserved it."

"So is that the reason why you were at the graveyard in the rain about a month ago?" He questioned, his mouth forming an 'o' shape. "I'm so sorry for what happened to you."

"Yeah, that's why I was there. And . . . it's okay. I've dealt with it for the past few years," I shrugged it off. "Anyway, aren't your parents still together?"

"They are," he replied nonchalantly.

"You're so lucky. I wish my parents were still together. I wish even more that my Dad was alive right now," I exhaled. "Too bad that can't happen."

"It may never happen, but at least you still have your mother, right?" Elias reasoned, his thumb brushing on the rim of the table.

I nodded, but inside, I still wished that my Dad was still alive more than anything. It's all I've wanted for the past few years. It's a wish upon a star, one that will never come true.

"That's reasonable. At least you still have friends like Nora . . . and Cannon and I if you count us as friends," he said.

"Yeah . . . you're right. I guess I can count you two as my friends, and Nora, of course," I stated. "You're an interesting person, Elias. I like you."

"You're interesting, as well," he hummed.

I wasn't lying when I said that. Something about Elias is interesting, but I just haven't figured it out yet. It hasn't unfolded, and probably won't anytime soon, but he's intriguing. I actually like it.

14. Future

ELIAS

AFTER SCHOOL, I found myself in the art room, a canvas laid on an easel. It's the same canvas I'll be using for my TCVA entry, so I can't mess up. This is valuable to me, so I have to take my time and try not to get sidetracked. To my benefit, there was no one in the room. Ms. Edwards abandoned the room to pick up a package from the main office and all the other students went home. At least, that was what I assumed until I heard two feet march down the hall, giggles amongst themselves.

Axel and his girlfriend, Adrienne, showed up at the door frame. I wasn't surprised at all, considering that Ms. Edwards did say that we could stay after school whenever we wanted to work on our contest entries. However, I didn't want any distractions. Today is my first day of working on my actual painting, so it will be a day that will probably set the tone for the rest.

"Hi, Adrienne. Hey, Axel," I waved, setting down a sketch pencil to a nearby table.

Adrienne waved back with a genuine smile, while Axel cleared his throat. "Hi, Elias."

"So did you come here to work on your painting or something?" I questioned out of curiosity, my fingers clutched.

"No, I actually came here to check out some of the paints Ms. Edwards has so I can envision what I want for my painting," he explained nonchalantly. "I'll start my painting soon, though."

"Uh, okay. All of the paints are stored back in the storage closet, though. I don't know if the door is locked or not," I gestured to the closed door with a shrug.

He slowly approached the door, his girlfriend trailing behind him. "It's open." They both disappeared into the closet and I turned back to my canvas, my finger planted on the tip of my chin. I was hesitant on what to do first, so I transferred the canvas from the easel to the nearest table to sit down and think. It would've been reasonable if I started with the body, and then worked on the features. There really wasn't anything else logical enough to start working on, considering that I'll need the person to show where the background will be. Suddenly, muffled conversation pricked my ears. It wasn't from the storage closet. It actually was from the hall.

Instead of minding my business, I listened. The voices sounded familiar, but I couldn't pick up on the conversation they were having. All I knew was that it was Rylie and Ms. Edwards speaking. Once they entered the door of the room, I realized I was correct. The two lugged one box each in their hands. Presumably, they were some type of delivery.

"Rylie, thank you so much for helping me with these," Ms. Edwards acknowledged as she stacked the boxes on top of each other on the floor.

"I-It's no problem. I had to come back here because I think I forgot something here, anyway," Rylie reasoned.

"I'm going to place them inside of the storage closet," Ms. Edwards picked up all three boxes at once, leaning to the left to see where she was going. "The doors should be unlocked."

"It is. Axel and Adrienne went in to see the paints you had," I stated, rushing up to the door to open it. She went inside and I followed. Axel wasn't lying when he said he was looking at paints. He was looking through each and every color he could possibly find on the shelves. Adrienne helped, but pretty much only with pink.

"Is there a specific color you're looking for?" Ms. Edwards questioned, her eyes lightening up.

"No, I'm just trying to get an idea of what colors I'll be using for my contest painting. That's all," Axel cracked a smile.

The teacher nodded as she dusted her hand. She dragged a wooden door stopper to hold the door open with her feet under the door before she abandoned the room to go to her desk. Maybe I should've been looking at paints as well, but there was no use of it now. I left the closet to go back to my canvas.

Before I got the chance to pick up my pencil, Rylie approached me and took a seat at the table I was at, a book that she didn't have when she entered the room by hand.

"Hi," I looked up from the canvas to face them.

"Hey," her tone matched mine.

Instead of attempting to continue to figure out what I was going to do on my canvas, I muttered. "So, has Nora figured out which design you're going to make her scrunchie out of yet?"

"She has," she muttered nonchalantly. "She plans on using the silver satin material. She thinks it'll be a great accessory for a Halloween costume or something. Speaking of that, will you dress up as something for Halloween?"

"I don't know yet, but maybe," I shrugged.

Rylie nodded in response. Referencing my current situation, I wouldn't have the easiest time figuring out what I would do. I knew what to do, but I was perplexed on what to do first. My canvas was still blank, and the tip of my pencil was still as sharp as a needle. I couldn't keep staring at the canvas for the rest of the time I have here at school. I'll have to get to work soon, so I picked my pencil up and started with what was most reasonable, the head and body and picked it up from there.

It was yet another typical day at Taco Fiesta. There were hardly any customers and the sales were quite low. I spent most of my shift time sitting down, waiting for customers to serve. From the break room area, I overheard my boss and the establishment's owner, Mr. Mercado, and his wife speaking about the future of the restaurant. It wasn't pretty, that's for sure.

They discussed that there was a possibility that their business may or may not close within the next year— maybe earlier. This made my heart drop. I've practically grown up in this place. Every time I walk through the doors of this establishment, I feel nostalgic. I came here as a child on a normal basis. I could never imagine this place closing down.

So, of course, I commented on the situation. I couldn't resist it. I just couldn't.

"You can't close down this place, you just can't," I protested. "It's too good to be closed."

"I know, but it may be the best decision. Our sales have been declining more and more," Mr. Mercado sighed while rubbing his forehead with a damp cloth.

"What if we find some way to promote the business? I'm sure there's some kind of way. I can help, too," I suggested.

"I appreciate you willing to help, but please don't strain yourself," he said, his head shot down the the ground. "Everything will be fine, I promise."

Come to think of it, it may have been the best decision to close the restaurant, but were there ways to promote their business so the sales can go back up? Possibly, there were. If we had an ad for the restaurant, it wouldn't be basic. Maybe we could promote it on Instagram or something. I wasn't much of an expert on Instagram or it's algorithm. I didn't have answers, but I certainly was interested in finding some.

The future of Taco Fiesta was declining, and I can't let it stay like that. In order to bring everything back up, I'll need help. Fortunately, I already knew who to contact.

//

Hi! Thanks for reading!

I've been so busy lately, but I hope you all have been doing well.

15. Connection

RYLIE

FRIDAY MARKED THE last day of homecoming week, and I've been spending it at the school's auditorium with my friends, somehow figuring out ways to save Taco Fiesta. Elias practically dragged us all down here to discuss what we can do to save the restaurant chain. Even if it would have to be a collaborative project, I was in for it. I couldn't bear seeing the restaurant closing down. I adored that place with all my heart. It brings back memories I'd never want to forget. So of course, when Elias consulted me about everything, I couldn't decline.

Nora was grilling Elias with questions about Taco Fiesta to figure out ways the restaurant could be promoted. Out of all four of us,

Cannon, Elias, herself, and I, she knew most about social media and its algorithm, so it's safe to say that she is a huge boost to what we have planned. Well, to be fair, we didn't have much planned yet. We were just getting started.

"Does Taco Fiesta have any social media accounts?" Nora questioned Elias as she typed something onto her phone. "I'm looking on Instagram right now, and so far, there's nothing for it."

"Yeah . . . there's no Instagram for the restaurant. In fact, I don't think there's any accounts for Taco Fiesta on any other platform, either," Elias replied with a grimace.

Nora started to explain how people paid all their attention to social media and the internet in modern times, not so much on paper or anything anymore. She reasoned that there would need to be a social media account set up for the restaurant to advertise the meals they serve. She suggested that it wouldn't be easy, considering that Taco Fiesta is a small business and only has one location.

It made sense. It would take quite some time for the social media posts to earn attention, but if everything is done properly, Nora says that the restaurant should gain some more customers.

"We can pull this all off, but only if we have nice pictures of some of the foods that are served at Taco Fiesta, along with some great filters, and maybe a bit of editing for the photos," she hummed. "Oh, and I can't forget tags added to each post."

"I took photography in junior year as an elective, so I can take photos of some of the foods," Cannon recommended. "I can even help edit them."

"I can help with that," Elias offered.

"I guess I'll help with that, too," I gave in while biting my lip. I couldn't just sit and not do anything. It would be no help to the group, whatsoever. Even if this will require communication, I guess there's no other way to pull this off. It is what it is.

"That settles it. I'll manage the Instagram account, in that case," Nora announced with a grin.

Another voice from a distance away directed towards us. It was feminine, and was a bit familiar. To me, at least. "Hey, what are you all working on?"

From her features, I could tell who she was, but I wasn't too familiar with her name. I think her name was Adrienne or Andrea? I'm bad at names, but all I know is that she's Axel's girlfriend. Adrienne had her wavy, brunette hair freely draped on her shoulders. She wore sleek, black leather pants and a fuzzy, white sweater to match.

Nora was the first to respond. "Hi, Adrienne. We're working on promoting Taco Fiesta. Wanna help?"

"Sure," she smiled with glee, gesturing to her boyfriend who trailed behind her. "C'mon Axel, let's help."

He looked as if he just wanted to get back in his bed and sleep, but he mustered a sluggish smile. "Fine." They adjusted themselves and took seats in the row of seats in front of us.

Adrienne reached her hand to meet mines and mustered a genuine grin. "I don't think we've talked before, but I'm Adrienne. What's your name?"

"I'm Rylie," I extended my hand to shake hers, mustering the best smile I could in ages.

"It's nice to meet you," she beamed before turning to everyone else. "So, have you all made any arrangements yet?"

"So far, I'm in the process of making an Instagram account for Taco Fiesta. We're planning on posting pictures of some of their meals," Nora explained briefly, gesturing to her phone screen, which had the account setup page on it.

Adrienne nodded. "I suppose I can help by promoting the page on my account. It'll probably attract a bunch of teens like us, though."

"It'll be something, at least," Cannon shrugged. "We should meet at Taco Fiesta after school today to start taking pictures and get the editing process going. There's no time to waste."

Elias insisted that he'd be free, while everyone else said that they may not be able to make it for different reasons. Adrienne and Axel already had plans to go to the homecoming dance tonight and Nora had a dentist appointment and had to go to work afterwards. That left Elias and I to start working on the project.

I have no problem working with only him today. The less people to work with, the better. There wasn't much of an issue, really. This could give me time to hang out with him outside of school, at least. I was looking forward to it for the sake of Taco Fiesta. Hopefully, our plan will bring back customers.

After school, I headed straight to Taco Fiesta. The establishment isn't far from school, so to my advantage, I was able to walk here without taking too long. The downside is that I smell like outside. I sniffed the sleeve of my hoodie, only to find that I somehow smelled like grass. I went out of my way to shower and spray on plenty of perfume this morning. How was it possible that I already smelled like I rolled around in grass, like an overly hyper child?

I didn't have my own car, and it was completely unknown when I'll get one, so the only way I can get from places is to walk (if it's within walking distance) or to get a ride from my Mom or from a friend. I learned how to drive last year, and even have my license, but I still don't have my own ride. I wish I did, considering that I wouldn't have to depend on others for one.

Referencing my current situation, I was inside Taco Fiesta, searching around to see if I could find Elias anywhere. All I saw was the golden yellow hue of the walls with tiny sombreros plastered across it. Finally, I spotted him at a table with his backpack, a camera in one hand as he tapped the table with his fingers with his other hand. I approached him, my mouth dropped open as I stared at the camera.

I didn't quite expect him to show up with that. I expected for us to take pictures with our phones, edit them, and post them on Instagram. I guess my expectations were low.

"Hey, Elias. I see you came here with a camera," I planted my hands on my hips, still kind of surprised.

"Yeah, it'll give us decent quality. Mr. Mercado, the owner, agreed to lend this to me," he explained as he rose up from his chair. "We'll be taking pictures back in the break room for a bit more space, if you don't mind."

I nodded as he gestured to me to follow him out into the back. We went behind the counter that contained the cash register and other necessities. I followed him into a small hallway that led to what appeared to be the break room. A man, who I assumed was the owner and a woman, who probably was his wife, were making adjustments to a display they made on a long, folding table, which had white table cloth spread above it. On the table, there were tacos, burritos, quesadillas, nachos, and just about anything else you can think of to expect to be sold in a Mexican restaurant.

"Good afternoon," the owner smiled as soon as he saw me. "I'm Miguel, and this is my wife, Isabella."

Isabella grinned with a wave after making one last adjustment to a taco. "Hi, sweetie. Thank you again for this."

"Really, thank you. You two didn't have to do this," Miguel acknowledged.

"We won't be the only ones working on this, but it's nothing. We just don't want this place to close down," Elias replied. "We can handle this for now, so you two can get back to the kitchen."

"Just holler if you need us," Isabella proclaimed before she gestured her husband back into the kitchen. Once the couple was out of sight, Elias and I were left alone. No one else was in the break room, not even any employees. It was just us.

I cleared my throat. "So, should we get started on the pictures?"

"Yeah, we should," Elias nodded in agreement as he turned on the camera. Before he could take pictures, he made a couple more adjustments to some tacos and burritos and observed what they looked like in the camera frame. Once everything was placed correctly, he took a couple of photos. While this happened, I started to adjust the quesadillas, enchiladas, as well as the cinnamon rolls. To add detail, I sprinkled basil from a small square-shaped bowl on and around the enchiladas and quesadillas.

"Thanks," Elias smiled genuinely as he took a few shots of the quesadillas and enchiladas separately. He also took a few pictures of the cinnamon rolls, his hands steady throughout the entire process. All the food that was on display was real and recently cooked, judging its appearance. It wasn't anything old. Once Elias took enough pictures for a start, he motioned back to the front area where he was sitting before I got here.

Without any questions, I followed. Once we were seated, he pulled out a laptop from his backpack, as well as a USB cable from the camera's case. "I'm going to upload the pictures onto my laptop so I can send them to Cannon to edit, since he's good at editing," he explained as he lifted the screen of his laptop.

"While you do that, I'll just start gathering all of the food in the break room," I offered as I got up.

"I'll be right there. This will take a minute or two," Elias said as he plugged in the USB cable.

I wandered back off to the break room and brought a small waste bin that was laying around towards the table so I could dispose of the food. It was nearly cold and was touched, so there wasn't much of a point in saving it. Bit by bit, I scooped the food into the trash and swept the basil leaves from the table into the bin with my hand.

By the time I was done, there was only the tablecloth left. There weren't any stains on it, so I picked it up from the table, folded it, and placed it on a nearby shelf. There were foldable chairs standing around nearby, so I pushed them under the table one by one.

"I see that you're already finished," Elias said while he approached me. "So now what do we do?"

"I don't know. Maybe we can . . . stay here for a bit? If you want to, of course," I blurted out.

Okay, I have to admit that I would never have expected myself to just say that out of the blue. I'm not much of a social person, but asking him to hang out here with me was a bit much for me. Perhaps hanging out with people instead of sitting in my bedroom sulking was a bit of progress for me.

Goosebumps crawled on my skin as I waited for his response. "I can stay here for a little while."

He motioned me to a table in the front area. He sat on one side, and I sat on the other, so we were across from each other. At first, it was awkward. Neither of us said anything, up until he cleared his throat.

"Do you know what you want to be when you're older?" He questioned, curiosity gleaming in his eyes. "That's if you want to share, of course."

"I haven't figured it out yet, but I want to major in psychology. I'm fascinated by human behavior and mental processes, somehow, but I don't know what I'd particularly choose as a job," I grimaced.

"Psychology is indeed interesting, but have you figured out what exactly you want to do?" Elias suggested. "With a degree in psychology, you can become a counselor, psychologist, or something like that."

"Maybe, but I still haven't figured out what exactly I want to do. Thanks for the suggestions, though," I acknowledged as I mustered a smile.

"It's no problem," he hummed as his eyebrows danced.

After that, it was silent again. The only thing I could hear was the drink fountain making an obnoxious whirring noise like it usually does and music playing in the background over it. Elias was adjusting and began to adjust things inside his backpack while I just stared at him. Not in a bad way, but probably in a good way. He has nice, full eyebrows that are arched so nicely, yet they were completely natural. His forehead was covered by his naturally brunette curls. Come to think of it, I never actually took a good, detailed look at him. I have to admit, he looks kind of cute.

Right at that moment, he finished adjusting his things and looked back to me. My entire face heated up. I was perplexed as to why it did, but it happened. After a few long, awkward moments of silence, he started rambling and questioning me about future aspirations. We discussed and laughed a bit. It wasn't inappropriate and it wasn't boring.

It was normal.

16. Hope

ELIAS

PROCRASTINATING IS SOMETHING that I am a professional at. Multitasking, as well. I have an insane amount of homework to work on, but I pushed that all back to work on it later. Right now, I'm working on a drawing. Not my contest entry for TCVA, but something else. I'm doing this to free up my mind. Not because I'm going through any stress or anything, but just for fun.

Today was eventful. Rylie and I started our plan of advertising Taco Fiesta by taking photos of some of the food that are offered. Cannon said that he'd hopefully have the photos edited by tomorrow, which sets the tone off for the start of actually promoting Taco Fiesta. All day, I've been pondering on if our plan would work or not, but we'll have to see how it goes once everything falls in line.

Other than that, I got to have a conversation with Rylie—which felt mutual. It wasn't serious nor irrelevant. It was just a typical conversation about the future, which included aspirations, and simply, stuff about life. It was refreshing, especially since today was a train wreck. Between keeping up with classes and saving Taco Fiesta, it was gratifying to wind down for a bit. I felt different around her, not necessary in a bad way, but in a good way.

My thoughts were interrupted by a clamorous, recurring knock on my bedroom door. "Come in," I hollered as I turned my roller chair away from my desk, covering my sketchbook with my homework papers. The door opened slowly, making a creak noise. It was my mother, who was still in her work clothes, skirt and blouse. She had a mug in her hand, a tea bag hanging out from the side. I raised my eyebrow, wondering why she was here.

"Elias, I made tea for you," she chirped, moving a few papers out of the way so she could set down the mug. During that process, my sketchbook was shown, only to reveal a rough sketch of skyscrapers. Internally, I did a facepalm because she wasn't quite meant to see that because I was supposed to be working on my homework, not sketching.

"Wow," she observed the book. "This actually looks great."

"It could use some improvement, but yeah, I guess it looks okay," I shrugged as I curled my fingers around the handle of the mug to take a sip that hopefully wouldn't burn my tongue. A generous amount of steam rose up from the tea. It wasn't too much, but it wasn't a little bit either. I ingested a tiny sip as my tongue curled up. It wasn't as hot as a McDonald's coffee, which I hear is scorching hot, but the tea wasn't warm, either.

"So how has school been lately?" Mom questioned as she adjusted my opened blinds.

"It's been stressful, but on the bright side, I decided to enter a city-wide art contest," I replied, enthusiasm perking in my voice here and there.

"That's cool. What are the prizes?" She inquired.

"An art scholarship to Laurier University, a one-thousand dollar cash prize . . ." I tried to reflect on everything. ". . . and two summer tickets to Italy."

Mom held a hand over her chest in shock. "That's actually a great prize. If you win, who is the second ticket going to be for?"

I paused. "I . . . actually don't know yet. I never even thought about it, but I'm more excited about the art scholarship at Laurier. I hear they have a nice art program over there."

It was true. I didn't know who I'd give the second ticket to. I don't want to give my ticket to just about anyone. It'll have to go to someone special. Someone who I'd want to relax and spend quality time with. I could already get an idea of who I want to go with, but I probably shouldn't be jumping into conclusions right now. As of now, I'm genuinely more excited about Laurier and getting the chance of winning an art scholarship.

Let's be clear. Laurier isn't quite my dream school, but I heard that they have a nice art program. I just had to bring that to Mom's attention, considering that her and Dad can actually save some money, considering that college around here is not cheap. I began to explain to her how the art program would be beneficial to establish a stable career of being an artist.

Let's just say that she wasn't buying it.

"The program actually sounds nice, but I'm concerned about you being an artist. It's not a stable career, Elias, it really isn't. There is a chance that you'd make a good amount, but it isn't guaranteed," Mom explained.

"You're right," I accepted. "But what if I at least become an artist as a side job?"

"If the other job is stable, then I suppose you'd be alright," she planted her hand on my shoulder before she made her way to abandon the room.

I sighed before taking a sip of my tea, which was now lukewarm. There were hints of sweetness in it, but my tongue mostly felt the bitter flavor of the tea. What if Mom was right? What if I end up not making enough money—or even worse—none. Okay, maybe I'm over exaggerating, but my point still stands. At least, I think it does. I wasn't completely sure, and I wasn't going to spend the entire night thinking about it.

Unfortunately, I still have homework to work on, so I might as well continue working on it. I had work for Calculus and Literature, so I might as well work on Literature first, then work on Calculus. Even though my mind was setting up to think and process something completely different, my thoughts still invaded my head.

It didn't vanish. It just sat there.

Brisk, early morning air hit my cheeks as I trudged to the main entrance of school. It was still dark outside. The only lights that could be seen were lights from the school buses in the bus lane and lights from inside the building, other than the light peeking from the sky unfolding from sunrise. Dozens of students piled the broad sidewalk from the buses, chatting among themselves.

I, however, didn't have the motivation to do the same. It was six in the morning and all I desired to do was to crawl back in my bed. Today was nothing but a typical Monday where I craved energy that I didn't have. When I reached inside the building, I separated myself from the crowds of other students and rushed to the east side of the building to get to my locker. The corridor was just as loud and wild as a zoo. I unlocked my locker combination and took out my History textbook.

I felt sluggish, so I didn't shove it in my backpack. Instead, I hugged it with my arms before I took one last look at my locker. Papers filled with old sketches were so close to flying out. They made my locker look as if there actually weren't other items that were somewhat essential to school. The first bell rang as I slammed my locker shut. Before I got the chance to make my departure to first period, there was a brief tap on my shoulder.

"Good morning, Eli," Cannon gleamed from behind me, his phone in hand. "Guess what?"

"Good morning, Cannon. What do you want me to guess?" I mustered a smile as I raised an eyebrow, only because he seemed to have a lot of energy so early in the morning.

He powered on and unlocked his phone to go through his files to show me a few edits. "I edited the pictures you made for Taco Fiesta last night. Like it?"

As he scrolled through all the pictures, my eyes widened in amazement. The pictures actually appeared brighter and somewhat better, as if they were ripped out of a magazine. "I love them. You did a great job," I acknowledged.

"Thanks. I already sent the photos to Nora, so she'll handle them ending up on Instagram," he shoved his phone in his pocket. "So, how did taking pictures with Rylie work out? The photos did turn out nice."

"It was great. We got along well," I replied as if it wasn't a big deal. "After we took pictures, we sat at a table and rambled about life."

"That's cute. It sounded like fun," Cannon chirped as we entered homeroom.

"It was," I reflected on everything from Friday, a small smile spreading across my face.

All my classes before lunch period flew by within a breeze. Once it was lunch, we all gathered at a table in the lunchroom. Nora posted a picture for Taco Fiesta's Instagram page a few minutes ago, and we all showed some kind of enthusiasm for it. Already, the post had one like and the account had a follow. Probably because it was Cannon that liked the post and followed the account, but still.

Nora showed us her phone screen as another like appeared in her notifications. This time, it was from Adrienne, who was currently typing something into her phone. "I'm almost finished sharing this on my account. Hold on," she said as she continued typing away.

"That's great," Nora gleamed as she placed her phone face-down on the table. She opened a bag of Cheetos, foiled her hand into the bag, and inserted a chip into her mouth. The bright orange Cheeto dust was attached to her fingers, so she rubbed it off with a napkin. "By the way, Adrienne, where's Axel? Will he be joining us? He hasn't been here for the entire lunch period."

"No, he's actually eating lunch with his friends," Adrienne replied, her shoulders raised. "I just shared the post and it's already gotten a couple of likes."

"That's great. We're already making some progress," Cannon cheered as he reached out his hand to pat my back.

I mustered a smile. "Yeah, I'm interested in seeing how much this will help."

Hopefully, Taco Fiesta will gain some more customers just like it did in the past again. It's amazing how social media can be beneficial to pretty much anything, including advertisement. It may be surprising, but true.

Cannon, Nora, and Adrienne fell into a deep conversation about the post, which left Rylie and I alone. She was fiddling her fork around her lunch tray with one hand while her phone was in the other, scrolling through what appeared to be an e-book or something. She was reading, so I didn't bother her. I remained quiet.

On my lunch tray, I had a pizza crust, grapes, and a miniature water bottle. I took a grape and placed it into my mouth. It was naturally sweet and definitely not the best grape I've had, but it was alright. I inserted a few more into my mouth one by one. Before I could wash it all down with crisp cold water, a tap crept on my shoulder. Rylie's hand trembled as she set it down on the table.

"I was wondering... how did everything go with the Instagram post? I wasn't paying attention," she questioned out of curiosity with a faint chuckle, gesturing to her phone.

"Everything's starting out okay. Nora's post on the Taco Fiesta Instagram page has gotten a couple of likes, and Adrienne's post on her page also gotten some likes," he informed me, mustering a hopeful grin.

"Oh, that's cool," she muttered. "Also, if you don't mind me asking, how... is the painting going? Your contest entry, I mean."

"It's going great. I haven't quite started transferring everything to a canvas, but I have my sketch, at least," I explained. "I plan on starting on the painting after school today, probably at the lake in town . . . the same one where you made a suggestion for what I should paint."

Rylie mused, her mocha brown eyes glistening from the lunchroom's high-ceiling lights. "I know you can do it. Good luck."

I nodded in acknowledgement with a smile, looking forward to later on. I wasn't quite going to start painting, but I will decide what hues I should use and start drawing on the canvas before painting. It won't be anything some people would consider special, but it's something, at least.

17. Feelings

RYLIE

EVERYONE SCURRIED OUT of the lunchroom once the first bell rang like animals from the zoo. Lunch today was just typical. Nora posted a picture Elias and I took on Instagram and gained a couple of likes from it. During lunch period, Nora, Cannon, and Adrienne were chatting on and on about it, while I was sitting there, reading a book on my phone. I was irrelevant to the conversation anyway, so I figured that I should've stayed quiet.

That wasn't the case. I ended up talking a bit to Elias about his painting for a contest. It was casual and didn't feel so lonely. When lunch came to an end, we went our separate ways and I started my journey to my next class. It was Calculus and I didn't have a single friend there. I think Adrienne's in that class, but I never paid attention. I'll just assume that she is in the same Calculus class as me.

Speaking of Adrienne, she joined me as I prepared to walk up a flight of stairs, which left me dazed. Why did she want to walk with me?

"Hey," she beamed as she stood behind me while adjusting her brunette hair that was in a ponytail. "You're Rylie, right?"

"Yeah, I am," I confirmed, my hand wrapping around the rail as I climbed up the steep stairs, my legs already cramping. I was half convinced that the devil made them as a trap or something. It sounded childish, but climbing up and down these steep stairs is pain.

"That's nice. I just wanted to get to know you more. You're pretty quiet," Adrienne explained, her hazel eyes glimmering. "You do have Calculus for next class period, right?"

"I do," I said with a stammer. Instantly, I wondered why she was walking with me. I was used to walking from class to class with Nora, but then again, I hardly have any classes with her, so for some class periods, I walk alone. It's what I'm used to. Plus, why would Adrienne want to walk with someone like me? I'm almost positive that she has other friends that she can walk to class with. If not, she can walk with her boyfriend.

She reversed the topic as we reached the top of the stairwell. "How have you been doing lately?"

"I've been okay, I guess. What about you?" I asked in response.

"I've been alright. I'm all over the place right now . . . but I'm still okay," her voice sounded a bit shaky as she mustered a smile.

I took a quick glimpse at her. She was smiling, but underneath, I felt some kind of feeling that her smile was fake. Something could've been bothering her at the moment, but I had no clue what. Maybe I'm wrong. Maybe I'm just overreacting. That isn't any of my business, anyway, so I shrugged it off.

We walked through the crowded corridors as the warning bell rang. It was wildly loud in the hallway, but between Adrienne and I, it was quiet. Neither of us said anything. Not like I'd know anything to say that would break the chain of silence, so she saved the day.

"It was nice talking with you, Rylie," she smiled as we approached class.

"Same to you," I nodded.

As I entered the classroom, I sauntered to the back. The room was half-full with students, who were chatting among themselves and the teacher was nowhere to be seen. As I took a seat, I reflected on the last few minutes and speaking with Adrienne. She seemed sweet, however, something about her seemed off, like broken glass.

I had no clue what it was, but it was quite intriguing.

After school, I headed towards the lake in town to hopefully cram some information into my brain for an upcoming exam. I settled to study outside just to get some fresh air, since I'm awfully inside a lot. In case Mom would be mad at me when I came home, I texted her that I wasn't going to be home for another hour, maybe two.

I knew that Elias was going to be here, according to what he told me at lunch today. He'll be working on his painting and I'll be studying, so we'll both be focused. Speaking of him, I could already see him as I neared closer to the lake. He was seated at a picnic table that was a distance away from the water.

The bristles of the juniper green grass I walked across brushed against the bottom of my shoes as I neared the table. Elias looked up, a welcoming smile spreading across his lips when he saw me. He set down his pencil as he pulled his canvas that was laid flat on the table towards him so I could have space for my belongings. I mustered a warm smile. "I'm sorry if I bothered you from coming here. I just needed somewhere to study and I didn't want it to be at home," I apologized as I took a seat, setting my backpack on the bench beside me.

"No, it's okay. I'm not bothered at all," he insisted as he picked up his pencil again. We were directly across from each other, which gave me the opportunity to see him drawing. Although I wanted to watch, I had to get done with studying, so I removed my binder from my backpack and took out a couple of papers from the rings so I could read over them.

At first, I was focused. The sharp aroma of the pine trees tingled my nose as the noises of flocks of birds heading north for migration chirped, guiding me to stay on task. I did pick up on some information, but I became bored as I continued to read through my papers. It was tedious and I already felt like moving on to something else. Instead of automatically giving up on studying, I took a peek at Elias' canvas. It was upside down from my view, but based on what I saw, he drew a person and was drawing various leaves in the background.

Yet again, I was fascinated on how he could draw so well and be so focused. It was like nearly every move he made with a pencil in his hand was excellence. Was it magic? It wasn't, but it was pure talent. His head shot up from his canvas, his umber eyes gazing into mine. It looks like I got caught staring for a bit too long. "You've already finished studying?"

"No, I just got sidetracked by you drawing. It's a lot more intriguing than studying, for sure," I joked as I straightened out my papers. "You draw so nicely."

"Well, thank you," he acknowledged as he turned back to his canvas.

"Mhm," I hummed as I sluggishly stared at my papers to get back to studying. I practically forced myself into reading over the information. It was tedious, but it has to be done. Before I could keep going, my thoughts were interrupted, but I didn't mind.

"So, Halloween is around the corner. Do you have any plans?" Elias questioned as he looked up from his canvas, a small smile spreading across his face. "Or plans for anything coming up?"

"No," I blurted out. "What about you?"

"I don't have plans, either. Maybe we can . . . hang out? You know, a casual hang out," he suggested, his hand combing through his moisturized, brunette curls. "Only if you're down for it."

"Sure, of course," I said the unthinkable. "What day?"

"Maybe sometime next week? Sometime after school, maybe? If you want, we can hang out at my house," he suggested. "As friends, of course."

"Sounds like a plan," I confirmed. "I'll need you to text me your address or something, through."

"Okay, hold on," he said as he took out his phone from what seemed like his pocket. After a couple of moments, he handed it to me so I can enter in my information. I typed in my name after I typed in my phone number and saved it into his contacts. I made a mental note to add him to my contacts once he texts me his address. I returned his phone, slightly looking forward to hanging out with Elias.

For quite a long time, I was always the one to lock myself in my room and isolate myself from the world. However, this time, I felt different. It was like a rope that was steadily unraveling, strand by strand. I didn't quite feel like isolating myself from everything and everyone anymore. I was still my quiet self, but I somehow didn't have a huge desire to be hidden.

It was baffling and difficult to break down. I had questions, but there were no answers. The inquiry will probably sit in the back of my brain for a long time. I guess it won't hurt to try to figure it out on my own. Right?

Since school started, I started to come out and actually do something less. Sure, there were times where I stayed in the comfort of my room and just sulk, but I shockingly made two new friends and hung out with them for a reasonable amount of time. Technically, I have hung out with them along with Nora outside of school at Cannon's house, and that was just last week.

Alongside that, I did spend quite a handful of time with Elias, like when we took pictures for Taco Fiesta, or the few times during lunch period where we would just . . . be normal people and talk. He's so refreshing to talk to. It's not that I don't enjoy talking to Nora and Cannon— I do. It's just that Elias is . . . different. Elias made me feel so . . . different. He made me feel a way I haven't quite felt before.

I was completely unfamiliar with the feeling. I couldn't put a finger on what it was.

18. His Heart

ELIAS

ONCE I TOLD Cannon about Rylie and I planning on hanging out tomorrow, he was ecstatic about it. For the entire afternoon, it was pretty much all we talked about. I wasn't shocked about it in any way. Knowing Cannon, I expected it. He wants to know every detail he can get about it, and I don't blame him.

"Do you, you know . . . like her?" He teased as he made kiss noises.

I didn't respond right away. It's the end of the school day and I'm already being interrogated with questions. I looked up to the baby blue sky to see puffy, pillow-like clouds dotted across as I pondered on his question. I was stumped on what to think. Even worse, I was stumped on what to say.

If I'm going to be honest here, I like Rylie. I like hanging out with her and I like talking with her, even if she doesn't talk that much. She's a nice friend and a great person. However, I can't figure out if I like her in that way. Feelings are just too confusing. I mean, she is cute and I like her personality. I enjoy talking to her—I really do.

Is it possible that I liked her in that way? Maybe, but I don't want to rush things. I still enjoy just being friends with her and I don't want to lose that.

"I don't know, man," I replied to my best friend as we entered his raven black Mercedes Benz. "Feelings are so confusing."

"Honestly," Cannon agreed while practically tossing his backpack into the backseat. His car was nice, inside and out. I didn't have a ride on my own just yet, unless you count me borrowing my mom or dad's car to get around. "What will you two be doing on your date?"

"Cannon, it's not a date," I rolled my eyes playfully as he drove way too fast out of the student parking lot. At this point, we were practically at risk of bumping into the curb, or worse, driving over it to hit a sign or something. "You're a horrible driver."

"I know, but don't use this as an opportunity to change the topic," he smirked as he turned around a corner, causing me to suddenly lean to the left. "Seriously, though, what are you two going to do?"

"We're going to hangout at my house. It'll be casual," I said. "My mother will probably insist on her staying for dinner, so she probably will."

"That's cute. What are you going to wear?" Cannon interrogated, taking a quick glance at me. I could practically see question marks shooting out of his eyes.

"I . . . haven't decided yet. I mean, it's not too much of a big deal, right? We're just hanging out," I murmured. Cannon let out a disappointed sigh while shaking his head. He looked as if he wanted to do a facepalm. I grimaced as I looked out the window, automatically seeing storekeepers removing Halloween decorations from the windows of their stores and replacing them with ones that were autumn-themed, specifically for Thanksgiving coming up in a few weeks.

"It's kind of a big deal, Eli. What you wear does matter. It's a make or break kind of thing," he explained as he stomped on the brake too hard, causing me to lean forward against my seat belt. If only the light hadn't turned red. "Since it's a casual occasion, you can just wear whatever. However, if it were more . . . formal . . ."

Let's be real. Cannon knows a lot more about what to wear to a certain occasion than me. This scenario is a perfect example of it. He isn't crazy about it to the point where he'd drag me to the mall to pick out something fancy, however, he will give certain advice that he believes will help.

"Does a nice sweater and jeans sound okay?" I questioned. I needed a second opinion of it just in case.

"Yeah, that'll be fine. Just make sure it matches and has no wrinkles," he replied. It was common sense. I wasn't going to wear anything mix-matched to any occasion, really. Unless you count several occasions of me wearing mix-matched pajamas to sleep at night. That didn't matter, though.

Once we pull up at my house, Cannon parks on the left side of the driveway due to my dad's car being in the way of the right side. "Bye, Eli. See you tomorrow," he gleamed, unlocking the car doors so I could make my departure. "Make sure to tell me all about your date with Rylie tomorrow night."

"For the love of God, it's not a date, Cannon," I rolled my eyes playfully as I nudged his arm.

"Keep telling yourself that," he tutted.

I said one more goodbye as I abandoned his car, my backpack tossed on my back. I sauntered towards the house as Cannon started to drive away. Once I got inside the house, I slipped off my shoes and placed them at the foot of the stairs so I could take the pair up to my room later. "I'm home," I hollered, placing my backpack on the floor beside the couch. Mom and Dad were in the living room watching something on our television while pretty much cuddling. Up until they saw me, at least.

"Elias, hey," Mom gleamed. "How was your day at school?"

"It was okay," I shrugged as I walked off into the kitchen meters ahead to grab a snack.

"That's great to hear, son," Dad said as he turned back to the TV to adjust the volume.

I opened the refrigerator in hopes that there would be something I desired to eat, but instead, I saw leftover fried rice, baby carrots, orange juice, ham slices, bread, and dozens of vegetables and fruits. I closed the door shut and opened it again in hopes of something else magically appearing. To my disappointment, nothing happened. Instead of walking off to the pantry, I took out the pack of baby carrots and put several of them into a bowl. It was better than nothing.

I joined my parents into the living room once again. I needed to tell them about Rylie coming over tomorrow and I was clueless on how they would react to it. I don't want them to get the wrong idea or anything. Her and I are hanging out as friends, and maybe they'll assume that we're more than that. No matter what, I just want them to approve of her.

"So tomorrow, my friend is coming over," I gathered all my courage as I bit my lip, slouching into the accent chair near the sofa my parents were on.

"Is it your friend Cannon?" Mom questioned, her eyes lightening up. "He's so sweet."

"No, not him. Another friend," I corrected. "Her name is Rylie."

"So it's a girl, eh? I see you, son," Dad smirked. He was already getting the wrong idea. "You're growing up so fast. It was like you were in diapers just yesterday."

My hand swept across my face, my face warming up. "No, Dad, we're not dating or anything. We're just going to hang out like normal people."

"If you say so," he shrugged with a wink. I rolled my eyes as I shook my head before taking a bite of one of my carrot sticks. Telling them both about Rylie coming over wasn't too difficult. Unsurprisingly, Dad did take things the wrong way, but it's all good. I had no worries about that whatsoever. The real deal to worry about was my dad embarrassing me in front of Rylie like this. I gulped at the thought. It was more than likely to happen, but I'll be just fine. Right?

During art class the next day, Ms. Daniels taught us about collages and the art in them. It's pretty much what she's been teaching us for the past few days. Today, however, we'll have the opportunity to take that into action. We're supposed to use an 8.5 by 11 inch piece of paper and paste various small photos to make one meaningful art using old magazines she has available at every table.

The assignment itself wasn't difficult. So far, I've stayed productive and found plenty of pictures to glue to my paper, mainly pictures of buildings, trees, rivers, etcetera. Rylie, Cannon, Nora, and Axel, who were also at the same table as me, appeared to not have a difficult time with their collages, as well.

Cannon and Nora were in deep conversation about modeling television shows, like America's Next Top Model, from what it seemed like, and Rylie was basically third-wheeling, coming into the conversation here and there. Axel was basically multitasking between the assignment and typing furiously into his phone for what seemed like every few minutes, but since Rylie sat across from me, I decided to make a move.

"What's the theme of your collage? It looks cool," I admired, slightly getting up to get a good look at her assignment. Multiple cut-outs of books, pillows, coffee cups, and anything that could possibly be related to that were pasted on the paper.

"M-My collage just . . . has this calm theme with all the things I like when it comes to comfort. It's nothing special," she informed, sneaking a peek at mine. "I like yours. It's so colorful."

I looked down to my paper. Mine had various cut-outs of buildings and anything landscape related. It wasn't too appealing, but I liked it. "Thanks," I acknowledged. After that, it was silence between us. It was awkward silence, too. It can't be like this when her and I hang out today, and I think she realized it as well. She opened her mouth, but no words came out. Then, she placed a finger on her chin.

"I've been wondering . . . how exactly did you get into art? Like, what made you so interested in it?" She questioned, her eyes gazing into mine. It was direct eye contact.

"Art has been something I've been interested in since I was little. I liked the idea of envisioning something and putting it on paper, so I did," I explained, a hand brushing behind my neck. "No regrets."

"Oh, that makes sense. It was pretty obvious," she mustered an awkward smile. "I feel stupid for asking."

"Don't be. You were just wondering, so it's not stupid at all," I assured her.

She insisted, lifting her head up to look at the ceiling, paper honeycombs dangling down from it. "If you say so." She paused for a second, then looked back at me. "I'm looking forward to later on."

"I am too. We can talk and you can meet my parents and we can maybe watch some kind of movie," I suggested. "You can even stay over for dinner if you want."

"I think I'll have to check in with my mother for that, but I think she'll be okay with it as long as I'm back by curfew," she reasoned, flashing a grin to me.

"Well, my mother will most likely insist on you staying," I chuckled.

She rolled her eyes playfully. "Then I guess I should—"

That moment, the final bell rang. I could see a smile appear on Rylie's face. My face mirrored that smile. The school day was over and done with. I looked down at my collage, empty white spaces here and there. It was a no-no according to Ms. Edwards, since she wanted us to have our papers with little empty space. I would've been finished if I hadn't been so caught up in talking with Rylie to the point where I forgot to finish working. I guess I'm a bad multitasker.

"Class is dismissed, everyone," Ms. Edwards cleared her throat from her desk as she stacked a couple of papers. "You all can finish and turn in your collages tomorrow."

I reached down to my backpack, which was still on the floor and slid my collage into a plastic, standard-sized folder. After, I threw my backpack onto my back and gathered any paper scraps from the magazines—small or large—and cupped them into my hands. I didn't plan on staying long since I'll have to quickly finish my homework and start getting ready to hang out with Rylie afterwards, so I prepared to say goodbye to everyone at our table. Not to mention that I have to work on some kind of drawing to give to her later on.

"Bye, guys. I have to get going now," I cleared my throat.

Everyone else said their goodbyes as I got ready, but Cannon specifically winked at me. I knew exactly what it meant. It was his way of telling me good luck for later on—but more so to tell him everything that has happened after Rylie and I hang out. He's expecting to hear from me after, so I made a mental note to tell him everything.

I just can't contain my excitement for later today.

19. Get In, Loser

RYLIE

NORA WAS RAIDING my closet and drawers, from top to bottom and left to right. It was oddly satisfying to watch her toss pairs of jeans on her shoulders and hold up shirts, observing them while squinting without causing too much damage to my bedroom. School let out nearly three hours and Nora's been searching for nice clothes for around thirty minutes. My room was still in a satisfactory condition, minus a small pile of rejected clothes on the ground besides my full mirror.

Since we got here, we've been talking about the most random things you could possibly think of with the company of my pet cat, Cookie. She is laying in my lap, playing with one of her toys while I'm sitting on the edge of my bed. "How's everything going with the search, Nora?" I questioned out of curiosity while lightly massaging behind Cookie's ears.

"Well," she grimaced, "it's been tough since literally everything you own is a hoodie or sweater, but I'll find something."

"You're over exaggerating. I own quite a few other types of clothes as well," I rolled my eyes in a playful manner as I picked up a sky blue decorative pillow with my free hand and threw it to her.

"Okay . . . maybe I am, but there's not much variety in this closet," she proclaimed while rummaging through my closet. Nora picked up a scarlet red hoodie dress, which made my eyes widen as big as saucers. I forgot about it completely, like a computer drive that's been wiped clean. Just by looking at it, I remember purchasing it at the mall with my mom several months ago, but it's never been worn. The price tag that hung out from one of the sleeves was clear proof. "What about this? The temperature is getting cooler outside, but it'll still look cute?" She suggested while holding it up to her chest to observe it in the mirror.

"Eh..." I hummed with a frown. I didn't want to wear it since dresses were never my style. In my opinion, at least. "I don't know... I haven't shaved my legs or anything, so I guess I can't wear it."

"Excuses," Nora shook her head with a grin while hanging the dress back up on the hook. She tossed a pair of denim blue jeans on her shoulder and went back to searching—or pretty much hunting—for a top for me to wear. She unhooked one of my hoodies from its hanger and picked it up from the shoulder area on each side to present it to me. The hoodie was lavender purple and had the phrase, Mondays Suck over it. "How about this? It's simple, but it'll work."

"It's fine, I guess," I responded as I lifted Cookie off my lap to transfer her to my bed. "I'll go put it on real quick."

"Yay!" Nora squealed like an excited fan girl while handing the pair of jeans and hoodie for me. "Make sure you freshen up while you're at it. I'll clean up this mess I made in the meantime."

I abandoned my bedroom and scurried down the hall to the bathroom. I closed the door shut behind me, the sugary aroma of lavender air freshener prickling my nose. I quickly folded the clothes and placed them on one of the shelves of the storage rack placed above the toilet. I decided to wash my face first, since it was kind of greasy from being at school and all.

As I cleansed my face with my foamy face wash, the thoughts of how everything would go with Elias invaded my mind. He's sweet and I want to believe that hanging out with him will be fun, but what if it ends up being awkward? Since I'll be at his house, what if his parents don't like me for whatever reason? As soon as my face was rinsed and dried, I tried to shake off the thoughts by looking at the bright side. Maybe his parents are actually sweet like him. Maybe Elias and I will end up having a great time with no awkwardness to interrupt everything.

I smiled at myself in the mirror. This smile wasn't fake. It was real, probably the realest smile I've had in a while. After I put on a bit of my day cream and straightened out my eyebrows, I put my clothes on and transferred the ones I was already wearing to the laundry hamper at the corner of the bathroom behind the door.

I planted my hands on my hips and turned back to the mirror. I was ready to go, but my hair wasn't. Today, my loose curls hung freely above my shoulders. The part was closer to the side than it was in the middle, so I made the decision to slay a little bit of the smaller side back with gel and attach a pinky-sized white hair clip so it was ensured that it would stay. I observed it in the mirror with approval before I abandoned the bathroom to saunter back to my room.

The moment I got in there, Nora was cradling Cookie in her arms like a newborn baby while sitting at the rim of my bed. Her eyes lightened as she saw me, carefully placing my pet cat on the bed before rushing up to me. "Ry—you look so pretty!" She exclaimed as she clasped her hands together.

"I guess," I placed a hand behind my neck. "Do you think I'm ready to go now?"

"Yes, but do you have any perfume? It's just a last touch," she recommended as she scanned my dresser.

"I do. There should be a few bottles in the first drawer to the right," I replied as I extended my hand to reach the dresser. The bottle I grabbed was one of my favorites that I owned. It was from Bath And Body Works, so of course it smelled nice. I practically showered myself with the mist several times before placing the cap back on so I could return it to its original spot.

Nora smiled as she picked up her backpack from off the floor. "I think you're ready to go now. Do you need a ride to Elias'?"

I nodded yes. She suggested that she'll be waiting in the car for me while I made sure I have everything. I grabbed my purse from my bed and placed my phone inside, along with basic toiletries, like lip balm. I think I have everything now, so I filed out the door, waving a goodbye to cookie, who was playing with one of her toys. I still hadn't told my mom about me going over to Elias' house, so I made a mental note to tell her before I left.

She was in the dining room this time, typing something into her laptop as she spoke on the phone. Once she saw me, she told whoever was on there to hold on and placed it face-down on the clear, glass table. "Mom, I'm going to head out for a few hours to hang out with a friend. Is that okay?" I pleaded.

"I'm so happy that you're finally making more friends," she beamed. "You can—but as long as you're back by curfew and you tell me where you're going. Who are you going to hang out with, anyway?"

"With a friend from school. His name is Elias," I said as I clutched my fingers. "I'm going to his house."

"It's a boy, I see. Well, fine then. Just be careful," she squinted her eyes at me. "Be safe."

"Bye, Mom. Thank you," I acknowledged as I filed out the door. Outside, I appeared calm about it, but on the inside, I was internally dancing. Well, until a loud, blaring horn interrupted me.

"Get in, loser, we have to go," Nora chuckled a Mean Girls reference as she rolled down the window. I dashed to car as quick as I could to the passenger seat, instantly fastening my seat belt so we could pull out. "What's the address?"

"Hold on," I replied as I went through my contacts. I found Elias and revealed the address to open it in Google Maps so she could listen for the directions. According to it, it would take a few minutes to get to his house.

As we drove, I couldn't contain my excitement. There wasn't much traffic, so the drive was a breeze. From what it seemed like, the neighborhood right around the corner. Once we pulled up at it, I could see many houses that looked nearly identical, but were different hues from the window. We were directed to turn around a corner to the right to a house at the left side of the street.

"Bye, thanks for everything," I said when we pulled up at the house while opening the door.

"It's no problem, but tell me everything that happens when you get home," Nora grinned. I made a thumbs-up and abandoned her car. The house looked neat from the outside. There was a cute little garden with nicely-trimmed bushes in front of the porch. As I rung the doorbell, my hands began to shake. The what ifs I had from earlier began to invade my mind again. I shook my head in hopes to shake off the thoughts as soon as I heard the door unlock.

"Hello, sweetie!" A woman with brunette curls and caramel skin tone similar to Elias' exclaimed as she opened the door. "Come inside. Elias has been been expecting you." She held out her arms to give me a brief bear hug. This woman, who was supposedly Elias' mother seemed genuine. "I'm Rochelle, Elias' mom. It's a pleasure to meet you."

"H-Hi! Your house is pretty," I glanced at the decorated dining room to the right of the foyer. Each chair had a table mat, plate, bowl, cup, and silverware neatly placed in front of it. My eyes turned to the reasonable-sized foyer. On the beige walls, there were multiple photos of Elias and his family. A sense of nostalgia rushed up my veins. When my dad moved out a few years ago, she took down all the photos with my father in them. It pissed me off, but at least they're still in the photo album.

"Thank you!" She grinned. A man, who was supposedly her husband and Elias' dad walked to us from around the corner. For a dad, he looked cool. He wore a dark grey hoodie and jeans.

"Hello! You must be Rylie," he introduced as I nodded in approval. "I'm Elias' dad, but you can call be Allen." He looked towards the staircase, only to see Elias staggering down. "Elias, son, your girlfriend is here."

I raised an eyebrow while coughing. It wasn't a real cough—it was a cough to prevent me from laughing. The situation wasn't any better for Elias. He slapped a hand across his face while shaking his head. "Dad . . . she's . . . I . . . uh—" he stumbled on his words.

"We're really good friends, Mr. Greene," I interjected with an innocent smile.

"Allen," he corrected with a chuckle. "And sure, if you insist." He turned to his wife with a certain look, one that people do when they're hesitant about something. "Honey, do you think that we should let her stay for dinner?"

"Of course. I'll be finished preparing dinner soon. I hope you like lasagna, sweetheart," she beamed.

I nodded with approval, which caused her to flash a relieved smile before motioning Mr. Greene—or Allen, I should say—back to the living room. It was to probably give us a bit of privacy.

"I'm sorry about my dad. He's just . . . like that," Elias apologized, planting a hand on the back of his neck.

"It's completely fine. What do you want to do first?" I shrugged it off.

"How about . . . I show you my room? After, we can chill and watch a movie or something," he suggested. "Only if you want to, of course."

"Sure," I said as I let him lead the way. He was halfway up the stairs by the time I slipped off my shoes and placed them near the door. I caught up by running. Thanks to my mix-matched socks, I was at a lower risk of getting a rug burn. Should I have changed into matching socks? I should've, but hopefully, Elias won't care. He doesn't seem like the type who'd care about mix-matched socks, anyway. It's a normal thing.

Once we were in his room, my mouth dropped open as I walked through. His room was organized and his bed was made—probably cause he knew I was coming over, but still. There were three beautiful paintings on his beige walls with him, Cannon, and his parents. I didn't know he was that good of a painter.

"I love your room. It's so cute," I admired as I took a seat on his roller chair.

"You're the one who's actually cute," he shot back with a grin as he adjusted the sleeve of his scarlet red sweater. I couldn't help but laugh at his cheesy compliment. "By the way, you can sit on my bed if you want. I can get my laptop and we can watch a movie until dinner is ready."

"Sure. Wanna watch Mean Girls?" I suggested as I sat at the rim of his bed. I watched the movie a billion times already, I just wanted to enjoy it with him. He nodded yes as he grabbed his laptop off of his desk and placed it on his bed. He went on Netflix and hooked up the movie on there, placing it at full screen. We both made ourselves comfortable with pillows and a reasonable-sized, plush throw sheet.

As the introduction part of the movie rolled, I noticed that we were kind of far a part, and that was on my end, so I scooted closer to him. He smiled, his eyes twinkling through the light of the little sunshine that was left outside. "I've watched this movie with Cannon once. It was iconic," he remarked randomly.

"It really was," I grinned. "It's nice to watch it over again with you."

He nodded in agreement as he turned back to the screen. I was looking forward to the rest of day with no worries.

We were nearly halfway done through the movie when the aroma of lasagna coming from downstairs prickled my nose. It smelled amazing and was looking forward to taking a bite. I already texted Mom that I would be staying for dinner and she agreed, so I was all set. I was leaning on Elias' shoulder because I got kind of tired of watching the movie. He could tell, so he turned it off.

"Dinner smells good from up here. I can't wait to eat," I admired as I got off of his shoulder.

"It does. My mom will call us down when she's finished preparing everything," Elias informed me. "How do you like it here so far?"

"It's nice. I like your parents. They're cool," I replied.

"I'm sure that they like you, too. You're sweet, so I don't see why they wouldn't like you," he smiled, his face sort of reddening.

"Knock it off. The person that's actually sweet is you," I nudged his shoulder playfully.

Before he could say anything else, the sound of his mom calling us down for dinner ringed our ears. He got off the bed and held his hand out to help me down, even if it was unnecessary. We walked down to the kitchen table together like normal people. I nearly licked my lips while sitting down. The lasagna, which was in a pan, smelled mouthwatering and I couldn't wait to take a bite.

"Thank you for letting me stay for dinner," I acknowledged as Ms. Greene brought in cups for all four of us.

"It's no problem at all," she gleamed. "Now, let's dig in."

The food was more mouthwatering than I thought it would be. By the time I got through seconds, I was stuffed. Unlike at home, everyone interacted a lot, mostly Elias' parents. It warmed my heart with a sense of nostalgia because I hadn't felt like this in so long. Elias and I didn't talk much, but we did exchange friendly gestures to each other throughout the meal.

When it was time for me to leave, Elias offered me a ride home in his father's two-year-old Toyota SUV. As we left, Elias fished a folded wad of paper from his pocket and gifted it to me. I opened it with care, revealing a large, hand-drawn lavender peony. There was a lot of effort put into it, I could tell, so as a thank you, I gave him a warm hug.

"I love it, Elias," I whispered to him.

"I'm glad you do," he whispered back as his fingers brushed the hood of my hoodie. The feeling was different. I was completely unfamiliar with it, but I liked it.

Was I . . . falling for Elias?

20. Heartfelt

ELIAS

"I'VE BEEN WAITING all day!" Cannon nagged like a child whining for a toy, a little too loud for my liking. "Tell me about it all now."

I shook my head. Not in a disapproving way, but in a chill, playful way. "Quiet down, Cannon," I hissed while looking at our surroundings. "Everyone else is going to hear our conversation.

We were at Taco Fiesta eating enchiladas and burritos over lemonade. All day at school today, I refused to tell my best friend about everything that happened between Rylie and I last night. Not because I didn't want to, but because he'd get too excited. Leaving him hanging, however, was probably the worst thing I could possibly do. All because Cannon has been a little too loud, we've gotten a few dirty looks from strangers sitting at booths near us—but it wasn't as bad as I thought it would be. They were all complete strangers after all, some I've seen at school and such.

Taco Fiesta was gaining a couple of customers, more than usual. The restaurant wasn't completely full, but it wasn't empty either. Mr. Mercado was thankful for that and decided to treat Cannon and I to whatever we wanted. We told him it wasn't necessary, but he went out of his way to treat us, alongside Nora, Rylie, and Adrienne to a free meal. It was nice of him to do so, but in the end, all that mattered was the restaurant's doors being open.

I took a small sip of lemonade from my small-sized cup and looked up, only to find Cannon staring at me with a smirk. "I know, I know. I'll try to keep it down, but you need to tell me all the details about your little date, or whatever you want to call it," he insisted.

I began to explain from when my father embarrassed me by calling Rylie my girlfriend to her complimenting my room. I told him about my cringe-worthy, yet cheesy response to that and when we watched Mean Girls. She ended up leaning on my shoulder when we were like, fifteen minutes through the movie, so I was half convinced that she was bored.

Cannon insisted that watching movies can be kind of tiring. It made sense, so I nodded and continued informing him about yesterday. It was a success, really. My parents ended up liking Rylie, and she ended up liking them, so it was a win-win. Maybe I shouldn't be too focused on that, but I just want them to approve of her. However, what stuck out most to Cannon—and myself, if that counts most was when Rylie and I called each other sweet and when she gave me a hug.

The hug was cuddly and warm, as if I was hugging a stuffed toy. It only lasted a few moments, but anything that could possibly happen in a few moments can be significant, like a gem. The moment I called her sweet and she said it back was memorable, as well. I could've went on and on, but my mom called us down for dinner at that time. These two moments felt so special and new to me.

"Eeek! That sounds so cute," Cannon squealed like a helpless fangirl as he set down his half-eaten burrito. I pointed down towards the table, signaling that he should lower down the volume. "When y'all called each other sweet, you were totally flirting. Too bad you couldn't continue."

"I mean, it's okay," I said after taking another sip of my lemonade. It would've been nice to continue, but it's fine. "Anyway, what's been happening with you lately?"

"Well, a lot, actually. It's just the usual things, though," Cannon sighed as he dabbed the corner of his mouth with a napkin. "Over the last few weeks, I've met a few cool guys in class, one of them I actually liked. I found out that he was bi, but alas," he grimaced, "he has eyes for someone else."

"Aww," I said with sympathy. "You'll find someone one of these days."

"Yeah, I guess," he tried to lighten up by smiling. "I can't wait for Thanksgiving break in like, three weeks. My brother will be coming home for dinner this year."

"Wow, that's cool. Most of my family don't live around here, so we might as well come over as well," I said, which made him ecstatic. Cannon's brother is a college student. As far as I know, he only comes home at special occasions, like Christmas, Thanksgiving, and any other possible school break you could think of. I haven't seen him that much lately, nor do I know much about him. All I know is that he's my best friend's older brother, I guess.

When I got home from Taco Fiesta, I settled to my bedroom to work on my art contest entry. It'll be due in a little over a month, so I need to get everything done beforehand. My room was sort of messy, even if I cleaned it yesterday. My pajamas and a few T-shirts and all sorts of pants—from sweatpants to jeans—were scattered across the floor and my bed and my bed was unmade. My room typically looked like this, specifically on school mornings where there's a ninety-eight percent chance that I'm in a rush. The other two percent is where I be productive for once and decide to get up from bed the exact time my alarm clock rings.

The house was silent. Both of my parents were out at work, so it was just me at the house. It'll be beneficial because I won't have as many distractions, so I found a random five-hour fireplace noise audio on YouTube and listened from my laptop. You may call me weird for that, but the crackling sounds of fire is soothing.

So far, all I had left to do for my painting now was to simply paint it. Ms. Edwards was nice enough to loan me a few of her paints, so

I had everything I needed. I spread a bit of each color onto a paper plate and placed it on my desk so I can have easy access to it from my easel. First, I began stroking my paintbrush on the hair area with a chocolate brown color. It was relaxing to feel it glide across the canvas as I painted it, careful of that the paint wouldn't go around or below the hair area.

As I did this, my phone sang a brief noise. I gently put down my paintbrush to see what the notification was. "Rylie" flashed on the top of the screen. I clicked on it to see a text message from her.

Rylie, 3:55 PM:Hi! How are you? :)

This made me realize that we haven't talked much all day. I did see in her school, but we both didn't have the time to talk. I still had my collage to complete, so I had to stay productive. Not to mention that I decided to spend the rest of art to figure out colors to use for my contest entry. I wanted to at least get the hair done for my painting, so instead of texting her back, I FaceTimed her.

Within the third ring, she answered. I placed my phone on a porcelain white phone stand I had on my desk so I could see her as I paint. It looked like she was in bed, but she was wearing a grey sweater with Homer Simpson across the middle.

"Hey, I saw your text and I'm doing great," I finally managed to speak. "I figured that I call you instead since I'm actually painting right now."

"Oh, in that case, I'm sorry for bothering you," she apologized in an instant.

"No no, it's fine. I'll still get this done," I replied as I squirted some white paint on top of the brown so it could make a lighter hue. The bottle was nearly empty, so it ended up making an obnoxious fart sound, the same sound a bottle of shampoo would make when you're nearly finished with it. Rylie laughed a bit while I grimaced at what just happened, but I quickly covered it up with a smile.

I opened my mouth, but no words came out. Come on, brain. Think of something, already.

Before I could even think of anything, a muffled yell from a distance sounded from my phone. It was on Rylie's end, so she yelled something back. After, she turned back to me. "Sorry for that. My mom just got back home from work. She's literally always working," she rolled her eyes with a sheepish grin.

"It's okay. Is she anything like you? Like, quiet or anything?" I questioned randomly as I dabbed my paintbrush in my new mixture of paint. The moment I said it, regret started to rush through my veins. Why did I have to be so random and awkward at the same time?

"Oh, we're not alike. Not anymore, at least," she blurted as she sat up from her bed. "I used to be quite outgoing like she was, but everything—from the divorce to my dad dying fucked things up. Since then, I just wanted to hide by not being social. I've gotten a bit better, but the pain is still in me."

I put down my paintbrush and took a seat on my fake black leather roller chair. I couldn't just continue painting. It didn't seem right, considering the direction the conversation was going.

I never went through the tragic events she's been through, like having divorced parents or a dead parent. It sounded painful, and probably is more painful than it sounds. I could easily tell by the look on Rylie's face. She wiped a tear with the sleeve of her sweater as she sniffed.

"Out of all the people it could've happened to, it had to happen to me," she muttered. "I'm sorry about all of this—I really am. We can talk about something else if you want. You didn't have to stop painting because of me."

"No," I insisted. "My painting may be a priority to me, but that doesn't mean you aren't any less important." My face grew hot. "I don't know what all this feels like, but everything will be okay. Stepping out of your bubble won't be easy, but it takes one step at a time."

"I don't know. I still feel bad about everything that's happened, even if it's been a few years. I miss my dad and my parents being together . . . I miss it so much," she sighed as she cracked open a water bottle, a click noise sounding from it.

My hands trembled. This time, I didn't know what to say, and my brain wasn't being any help whatsoever. Again, I never experienced any of her pain, but I could feel it from the way she was talking. It was quiet, other than the sounds of fire crackling from my laptop. I paused the video and looked up at the ceiling in hopes that I'd figure out something to say.

"I basically spent my entire time in high school trying to figure out things, but I think this school year was the year where I actually took a few baby steps," she continued. "I made new friends and believe it or not, you've helped me step out of my comfort zone."

"I have?" I questioned, an eyebrow raised.

"Yes, you actually did. You know, all the times we . . . hung out. It was new to me," Rylie replied. "Thank you for everything."

"Rylie, it's no problem. I'm so sorry about everything that's happened, though," I said. "Seriously, if you ever want to talk about it, I'm here."

"Thank you. It felt good to get some things off my chest, but it took up your time and I'm sorry. I'll leave now, I have to work on my English homework, anyway," she reasoned.

"I still have plenty of time to finish my contest entry, so it's completely fine. I'll see you tomorrow at school," I said as I rose up from my roller chair, the bottom creaking a bit.

"Bye," she murmured before she hung up.

21. Be My Guest

RYLIE

IT'S BEEN THREE weeks since everything has happened. Three weeks since I went to Elias' house to hangout and three weeks since I figured it all out. I do—I most certainly do—like Elias Greene. I like how charming he is and how he's cute. I also adore how he's creative. I could go on and on, and that would take all day, however, that isn't quite the only thing I figured out.

As Elias and I talked over the phone three weeks ago, I came to realization about the unthinkable. This school year caused me to step outside my bubble, one step at a time, and it's all because I took Mom's advice to make new friends. I could hear her urging me to make friends through multiple occasions in my head. It was annoying, like mosquitos on a hot summer day, but I was relieved. Elias pretty much allured me to step out of my comfort zone through the multiple occasions of us talking. I grew comfortable with him over time.

And I'm grateful that I at least took a few baby steps. Even if I still feel the itching pain from the past, it felt good to try to move past it, even if it wasn't a lot. A little step could make a huge difference.

I pondered about this over and over again for the past few days. It wasn't a distraction to school at all because it is Thanksgiving break. It feels so refreshing to finally have a week-long break from classes, time-consuming studying, and exams where there's like, a forty percent chance that I'm not prepared for them. It's not necisarily a good thing, but I can fix that after the break. There's plenty of time, right?

My mom and I just arrived at Walmart. It's four days before Thanksgiving and Mom decided that it would be okay to do some last-minute shopping. Normally, we spend this holiday at another family member's house, but this time, Mom decided to flip the switch and invite some family to stay with us for dinner. I never liked large family gatherings, especially if it's over dinner, but this year, I'm stoked for Thanksgiving day. Hopefully, dinner won't feel lonely like it always does. I'm sure it won't.

"Aren't you excited, Rylie?" Mom cheered as we rushed past the Subway that was attached to the superstore. "Two of your aunts and uncles are coming over for Thanksgiving dinner. That means that you'll get to see your two cousins—Inez and Landon."

"Yeah, sounds great," I tried to get my tone to match hers. As far as I knew, Landon is only a year younger than me and Inez is like, a eight years younger than me, so I'm the oldest out of the two. Unlike me, they're both Archers. I haven't seen them in a while, so it'll be nice to see them, I guess.

We rushed passed all the fruits to to vegetables. Mom placed a few bell peppers into a bag and placed them in the cart while I grabbed lettuce. Once we had everything we needed out of the produce section, we headed towards all the meats. There was an entire seasonal section for turkey and by the looks of it, there were only a few left.

"Thank the Lord we got here before the store runs out," Mom said with a relieved smile as she picked one up to place in the cart. "Who knows? They may not have any more in stock since it'll be Thanksgiving in a couple of days."

I nodded at everything she said. Even if the store ran out, I wouldn't care that much. Turkey tastes dry to me, anyway—no matter how it's cooked. I guess I'm not a big fan of turkey.

As we strolled through the store, our cart got fuller and fuller. Just like the turkey, there were several other items that were nearly out of stock. Going Thanksgiving shopping four days beforehand isn't a smart thing to do, so I'll keep a mental note for that in the future. You never know when my mother will decide to do late Thanksgiving shopping again next year, or the year after that. I wouldn't be surprised if she did.

When we were finished with shopping, Mom decided to treat us both to a meal at Taco Fiesta. As we walked through the door, I smelled the mouthwatering, spicy aroma of food cooking in the kitchen. Elias was at the order station, like usual. Once we saw each other, I couldn't help but smile and he did the same.

"Why are you smiling at that boy?" Mom questioned, glancing at me as she took her cheap wallet out her purse.

"Oh, it's nothing," I was quick to say. "He goes to my school and we're friends."

I didn't lie about anything. I'm not that good of a liar. My mom hates when I hide things from her, as all moms do. She was the one who encouraged me to make new friends, so she'd probably shrug it off.

"Oh, alright. I'm glad that you're making friends," she flashed a smile to me as we neared the ordering station. Mom decided to do the unthinkable and introduce herself to him briefly, telling him basic information about her like how her last name is Archer instead of Henderson and how he can call her Madeline. Elias introduced himself as well, but since the conversation was going a bit off-topic, he questioned us what we wanted to order.

I craved hard-shelled tacos with a cinnamon roll as a treat, so I ordered that alongside a small orange Fanta. Once our orders were done and paid for, we sat down at a table near the door across from each other. It would probably take a few minutes for everything to be ready, so to prevent me from staring off into space, I took out Elias' drawing from my side pocket and gazed at it while straightening out the crease marks so it could like like it still was in good condition.

The peony was gorgeous, like diamonds in the sky as Rihanna would say. The petals were drawn as if it were a real flower. The way he colored it blew my mind even more. It was like I was staring at a real flower on paper.

"That's a pretty flower," Mom said as she placed her wallet back into her off-brand, caramel brown handbag. "Did you draw it?"

"No, you know I can't draw, Mom," I laughed as I took another glance at it. "Elias actually gave it to me a few weeks ago. He's a great artist."

"Oh, really? I can tell you like that boy. The way you smiled at him alone tells it all," Mom teased as she got up from the table. Elias recently called our order. "Just don't grow up too fast, Rylie."

"I won't," I promised.

"And tell me when that boy confesses his love to you," she smirked, causing a blush to creep up my face.

When it was Thanksgiving day, Mom practically rushed various places across the kitchen in a panic. It's been like this for the past few hours and probably won't stop for a while. The sharp smell of the turkey burning from the oven began to prickle our noses, causing

Mom to nearly drop the bowl of newly prepared salad so she could rush to the oven. She put on oven gloves while commanding me to step back, opening the oven with one hand. At this point, I was just surprised that the smoke alarms hadn't gone off yet.

The seasoned turkey wasn't in bad condition. It probably was a little over cooked, but I assume that it won't be too bad. In the oven, the turkey kind of looked like what you'd see on those cooking shows—the ones where they show you how to cook something gracefully, but in reality, it ends up being a flop.

Mom kept the oven open so it could cool down a bit before she would take it out of there. I didn't have much to do at this point, so with care, I placed our home-baked pumpkin pie on a porcelain cake stand and gently took it to the dining room, which was sort of next to the kitchen.

I placed the pie towards the middle of the rectangular-shaped, wooden table, next to where the turkey would be. The table still hadn't been set up yet, so I headed back to the kitchen to gather plates, cups, and silverware. Mom thanked me as I made several trips from the kitchen to the dining room to transfer everything safely. This year, we didn't have to worry about making the entire Thanksgiving meal since my aunts and uncles will bring food, but making the turkey alone seemed like a pain in the ass to my mom. Not to mention that she has to also prepare refreshments before everyone gets here.

As I set up the table, my phone vibrated from my back pocket with it's usual ringing notification noise. I stopped mid-sentence from arranging the silverware to see what it was. Elias' name flashed on my screen as my most recent message, alongside Nora and Cannon's name from a few hours ago. I tapped on the message within an instant.

Elias, 5:57 PM:Happy Thanksgiving, Rylie! Are you about to start dinner soon?

Me, 5:58 PM:Happy Thanksgiving to you too! We might start dinner in a half hour or less. It depends on when my relatives get here. What about you?

Elias, 5:58 PM:Around here, we're about to start in a minute. I'm at Cannon's house right now, so I'll message you later. I hope you have a nice dinner :D

Me, 5:59 PM: I hope yours is nice too :)

I placed my phone back into my pocket and went back to setting up the table. Arranging plates, cups, and silverware in an orderly way wasn't too hard, so I completed the task within the next few minutes. That's when Mom came in with the bowl of salad—the same one she nearly dropped several minutes ago—and a tray filled with separate small bowls various salad toppings, like croutons, tomatoes, and baby carrots.

Everything was placed on the table accordingly, not taking up too much space since there was still more food to be put on the table. As I settled towards to kitchen to get salad dressing, the doorbell rang twice, the high pitched bell ringing in my ears.

"Rylie, can you get the door? I'll be right there," Mom hollered from the kitchen as I sauntered towards the door. I looked through the tiny eye hole towards the top of the door to see Uncle Jared at the door with Inez, while everyone else was helping unload food from the van.

"Hey, Uncle Jared! Hi, Inez," I plastered a smile across my face as I gave them both brief, individual hugs.

"Hey, Rylie. How the heck are you doing?" Uncle Jared questioned with a broad grin.

"I'm doing great. My mom is out back in the kitchen, in case you were wondering," I suggested. He nodded as he went through the foyer to the kitchen. Inez stood there innocently before she asked me where the bathroom was. I showed her the way to the downstairs one as Mom came into the foyer to join me at the door.

The rest of our relatives were flowing into the house, hugging each other and catching up. I was shocked that both families managed to arrive at the same time, considering that they both live on opposite sides of the county. As I took off my apron, my other cousin, approached me, his cell phone in hand.

"It's been a while, Ry," he proclaimed as he patted my back. "How has everything been?"

"Everything has been fine," I said as Aunt Gabrielle, Uncle Jared's wife, approached us. She remarked how we both grown so fast, even if I haven't grown an inch and hugged us both tightly separately. I managed to escape to the kitchen a few minutes later to put back the apron and adjust my outfit.

It was a cider orange sweater an a brown, fake leather skirt that Mom bought and practically forced me to wear for dinner. I wasn't too happy about that, since I absolutely despise skirts, but I had no choice whatsoever. When I reported back to the dining room, Inez, her mother, Aunt Gabrielle, and Aunt Emily were already seated at the table as Uncle Jared carried the turkey there. Mom went upstairs to get changed, so when she got back a few minutes later, we were ready to start dinner.

I decided to eat a slice of my Aunt Emily's lasagna and string beans and mashed potatoes to the side. Taking a bite of the lasagna took me back to night where I had dinner with the Greenes. Aunt Emily's lasagna was delicious enough for me to take another bite, but Ms. Greene's lasagna tasted better in my opinion. However, I set that aside as I dug into the food, listening to the conversation everyone was having.

"Inez, tell everyone about how you won your school's talent show the other week with your amazing singing," Uncle Jared insisted to his daughter, a broad grin spread across his face.

"It's nothing, really," she insisted before she took a sip of fruit punch from her cup.

"To you, it's not, but she did fantastic while singing. You should've seen her. I have a video of it on my phone if you want to see it," Uncle Jared boasted.

"Show us after dinner, bro," Mom said as she drizzled caesar dressing over her salad.

Dinner passed by within a breeze. My aunts and uncles kept on asking me how I was doing with school and everything. It was overwhelming kind of, but it was okay. By the time I was finished with thirds and dessert, I was completely stuffed and could hardly move. All the adults situated themselves in the dining room, chatting about the most random things, but Landon, Inez, and I gathered in the living room. Dinner didn't feel lonely for once. It was interactive and yet again, it made me feel nostalgic.

Landon was rambled over and over again about basketball to Inez while she stared at the television with The Simpsons on. I was just on my phone, texting Elias. I assume he's done with dinner by now since he technically started dinner before me, so he'll hopefully respond within a few minutes.

Me, 7:02 PM: I'm finally finished with dinner. How was yours? :)

I placed my phone face down on my lap, awaiting his response. I didn't expect him to respond right away, but I didn't expect him to take forever, either. Even if it's been a few moments, it felt like ages. When I heard the relieving ring come from my phone, I automatically read the message he left for me.

Elias, 7:04 PM: Dinner was great. I hope yours was nice, as well.

Me, 7:05 PM: Mines was okay.

Elias, 7:05 PM: I liked spending mine with my family, Cannon, and his family, but I honestly wish you were there.

Me, 7:06 PM: Yeah, that would be nice. At least we'll get to see each other and the others when we get back from break this Monday.

Elias, 7:07 PM: Mhm. I have to get going home now, so I'll talk to you later. Have a good night later! :)

Me, 7:07 PM: Same to you, Elias! :)

I put down my phone with a heartwarming smile. Even as we texted, I could feel butterflies flow freely through my stomach. This was a series of more feelings that I keep to myself. I haven't told anyone about liking Elias, not even Nora, maybe because I don't know what to do about it. All I wanted was for Elias Greene to know that I like him.

Too bad it's easier said than done.

22. Drama

RYLIE

EVEN IF IT'S been a day since we all gotten back from Thanksgiving break, I was already dreading it all. I was dreading exams coming up and all the tiring assignments I'd have to do before the semester closes for winter break. I was also dreading the pressure to study all the information that has been learned this entire semester—especially the information that has been learned towards the beginning.

Things weren't any better for Elias, from what I could tell. Cannon, him, and I were situated in the art room as we watched Elias perform finishing touches to his painting. Nora would've came, but she had to help out with the theatre kids' dress rehearsal for their performance soon. It may be just me, but he seemed as if he was in a hurry—which wasn't a good outcome for what appeared on his canvas. It made everything seemed so . . . thrown together.

"What's the matter, man?" Cannon questioned to his best friend as he closed a textbook. "You seem like you're in a hurry." I guess I wasn't the only one that noticed his strange behavior.

"It's nothing. It's just that as I paint this, I keep thinking about how these last few weeks of the first semester are going to play out," he set down his paint brush on a circular paper plate, the same one he used for his paints. "Final exams are coming up, I have to get this painting turned in for the contest, and, you know, the usual end-of-semester stress."

"The last few weeks are pressure, however, don't rush things. When you finish with your last touches, I can drive you to city hall so it can be judged," Cannon assured him while combing a hand through his shaggy, lemonade pink hair.

"Take everything a step at a time. Breathe," I added while planting a hand on his shoulder. "There's still time for everything."

"Thank you both," he acknowledged with a relieved smile. It was a half smile. He looked back at his canvas and I did the same. It was more gorgeous than I could've ever imagined it to be. The colors he used were vivid, like colors of a rainbow, but better. His painting style seemed modern, but that didn't make it any less better. It was cute and way out of my league.

In my opinion, he was sure to win.

As Elias made his last touches, he got up from the table to dispose the plate filled with a colorful mess of multiple hues and to wash his paintbrush. When he came back, he wiped the table with a citrus-scented disinfectant wipe to clear any splotches of paint that unintentionally got on the table. I watched him gracefully glide the wipe around the table. I found it amusing for some reason, kind of like those hair videos on YouTube where people just do hair.

"I can't do this anymore," a voice trembled from the hallway. "I just can't."

My head shot up from the table. I gulped and exchanged worried glances with Elias and Cannon, who looked just as baffled as I was. I made sure to remain still so I could hear properly.

"But . . . do you actually want to end this now, Axel?" A desperate voice questioned. "Do you actually want to throw away our two-year relationship? Do you actually want everything to unravel?"

That's the moment when we all realized who it was. It was Adrienne. Axel and her were having quite a feud, a public one that was meant to be discussed privately. Maybe they thought that no one was around.

"Adrienne, I don't want to, but, I just can't do this anymore," Axel countered with a groan.

"Can we at least sort things out? I don't want our relationship to end this way—I truly don't," Adrienne sobbed.

"I can't . . ." Axel prodded. "We've did that so many times, but this time, it just doesn't feel right." I could hear sobs grow louder, then disappear into the opposite end of the hallway. Even if I only listened to the conversation, goosebumps crawled all over my skin. I could feel the tension by the way they were both speaking.

My heart ached, especially for Adrienne. We weren't friends—we were just two people who knew each other. Even if we're not friends, she was friendly to me the entire time we've known each other. It wouldn't have been right to stay here and think about it. I needed to check on her.

I got up and told the boys that I'd come right back and abandoned the art room. Axel stood in the broad corridor, kicking a paper ball to the other end of the hall. He noticed me walk by, but he didn't say a word. His face was reddened and swollen, as if he'd been crying. A few tears rolled down his cheeks, but he wiped each one away with the back of his hand. The break up had a heavy toll on him, even if he appeared to be the one who wanted to break up.

Adrienne, however, couldn't handle it, from what it seems. I didn't know where she could've gone, so I checked the ladies' restroom near the Fine Arts hallway. A couple of quiet sobs prickled my ears from a nearby stall.

"Adrienne? Are you there?" I murmured as I pushed the door of the stall she was in. Her head shot up as she dabbed her eyes with toilet paper.

"What are you doing here?" She questioned as more tears began to trickle down her eyes, like rain pouring down on a window.

"I came in to check on you. I heard everything..." I informed her as I snatched a few paper towels from a dispenser to hand to her. School toilet paper has always been rough. "Is everything alright?"

The answer to that question was obvious. No, everything was not alright, but I didn't know what else to say.

"No," she wailed as she put her head down. "I wasn't shocked about us breaking up or anything. We... haven't been on the best terms for the last few weeks, but I thought I could fix things. He doesn't want to get back together with me." She groaned as another wave of tears fell from her eyes to her denim blue jeans. "I love him, Rylie. I still love him."

I planted my hand on her shoulder and led her towards the sink. She blew her nose and disposed the wreck of snot-filled toilet paper and paper towels. Her eyes fluttered shut as she wiped her remaining tears with the back of her caramel brown hand.

"Everything will be okay. Axel may just want some space right now. We all need it every now and then," I tried to come up with the best advice I could think of. It sounded shitty, but truth to be told, I never been through a break up. Even if I was familiar with pain, I wasn't familiar with that kind of pain.

"But what if that's the reason why he broke up with me? He's probably tired of me," she countered as she shook her head, refusing to look at anything but the tiled, bathroom floor. "What did I do wrong? Was I a bad girlfriend?"

Those were questions I couldn't answer right away, so I remained silent until I could think of the best response. "I'm sure that the break up had nothing to do with those. It could've been because of something he's dealing with right now," I assured her. When you put some thought into it, that could've been why. Axel did keep on saying that "he couldn't do this anymore". He could've meant multiple things by that, but who knows?

The possibilities were endless.

Before I could say anything else, Adrienne reached out to give me a hug. Unlike my mom's hugs, they weren't tight. It wasn't loose, either. It was immaculate, so I hugged back.

"Thank you so much, Rylie," she proclaimed with a relieved whisper. "I'm so glad I have you."

I muttered a "you're welcome" before I abandoned the restroom to head back to the art room. To my surprise, Nora was there, alongside Elias, Cannon, and Axel. I guess dress rehearsals were finished.

Axel was sketching furiously onto a piece of paper with a mechanical, the led breaking several times before he gave up. He put his head down to the table, forming a fist with one hand to hit the table. The table didn't deserve any of this treatment. Nora sent me a worried look, signaling that they were trying to get him to calm down, but nothing was working.

I grimaced as I took a seat. Cannon patted Axel's back reassuringly and whispered that everything would be fine, but Axel's head remained on the table. "What a day," he said icily.

"You should probably head home," Elias suggested. "After all this, you need rest."

Axel rose up from the table, balling up his sketch of lines to make it into a paper ball. "I should, Eli, but what gives? Going home won't make my situation any better."

"What if you watch Disney movies while eating ice cream in bed?" Nora suggested. "It makes me feel better sometimes, but I guess this isn't the same scenario."

"It isn't... but thanks, anyway," Axel sulked as his fingers drew shapes across the table. "Thank you all." He muttered before he got up. He took one last glance at us before he abandoned the room. We all exchanged puzzled glances, but we all knew one thing.

This was the first time we've all seen Axel Hanson broken.

***

"It was surreal," I told Nora as we drove out of the school parking lot in her old Toyota Corolla. After Elias' painting dried up for a bit, him and Cannon headed towards city hall, while Nora and I decided to head home. For the past few minutes, I told her everything, from the argument to comforting Adrienne in the restroom. It was heavy, but she tried to lighten up the mood.

"I hope things get better for them," she sighed as she made a sharp right turn at a full stop. Her car let out a loud sputtering noise. The same one a constipated goat would, whatever that would sound like.

I nodded at her response as I stared out the window, seeing my own reflection through it.

"I can't wait for winter break," I said, breaking the silence in the car, other than the overly loud car engine hissing. "This semester was too much."

"Right, I can't wait to see what sales there's going to be at the mall and online," Nora brightened up. "There weren't that many good sales during Thanksgiving break. Maybe we could go shopping?"

"I'll see about that," I chuckled as she pulled up on my driveway. "Thanks for the ride. See you tomorrow."

"Bye, see you," she chirped as I made my departure, my backpack tossed on my back. I reached towards my front pocket for my house key. As Nora zoomed off, she steered around a car. I was baffled on if it was parked at our house or the neighbor's house, but that didn't matter. Mom normally didn't have visitors around at this time of day.

The atmosphere of the room was quiet to the point a pin dropping could be heard. I assumed that my mom was still at work, but she could've been taking a nap, also. When I looked at the dining room, I saw her purse and her laptop case, meaning that she was home from work. I went up the flight of stairs to her bedroom. I knocked on the door before I opened it gradually, the door making a creak noise through the process. That moment, I felt like a brick hit my head.

My mom was laying around in bed in a robe . . . with a man I didn't even know.

They were cuddling, but stopped mid-sentence as soon as they saw me. My mouth dangled open as my eyes widened.

"Mom?" I whispered in disbelief. "What are you doing? Who is this man?"

I had a countless amount of questions to fire at her, but the two I asked were what I managed to speak. She glanced at the man she was with with an apologetic look. The man had caramel skin tone and was wearing a porcelain white undershirt. He was a stranger and I was desperate to know who he was.

Mom's mouth dangled open, but no words came out, so the man spoke for her, his voice stuttering, "I should . . . probably leave. I'll take to you later, Madeline," he leapt out the bed.

You should. He grabbed his navy blue shirt and tossed it on alongside his matching jeans before he filed out the room with a grimace. It was just Mom and I, frozen like a glacier.

"Rylie..." She croaked as she got up from her messy queen-sized bed, adjusting her lemonade pink bath robe.

"What is it, Mom? Who was that man? Are you... hooking up with him or something?" I questioned in demand as my hand swept across my forehead.

"Rylie, the thing is... that man is my boyfriend... Kaden Casteen," she muttered.

I gasped. I knew something was off about that guy. Several weeks ago when Mom dropped me off at school, he called her. From what I recall, she insisted that he was just her co-worker. I guess this all explained the car outside, as well. I shouldn't forget the time where Mom said that she was going out to dinner with friends. Was she actually going out with this man? I bet she was, but who knows? It's amazing how I could be fooled so easily. It made me feel sick in the stomach, sick like the flu.

"Oh, I thought he was just your co-worker. That's what you said," I shot back as I felt my face burn.

"Rylie, please don't talk in that tone to me. I raised you much better than that," she demanded, flustered.

"Fine, but at least tell me how long you've been dating this Kaden guy," I shook my head as I planted my hands on my hips. "You left out the part that where he was your boyfriend on purpose."

"We've been dating . . . for almost a year," she reflected, closing her eyes with a grimace to prepare for whatever response I was going to fire back at her.

"You can't be serious, Mom," I dug my hands into my face. "You've been . . . lying to me this entire time. You never told me about this guy you've been dating. You just lied."

She paused for a second before she looked down while rubbing her temples with the tip of her fingers. "I know, and I shouldn't have, but I did it because I didn't know how you'd react."

"You can run, but you can't hide. The longer you hide the truth away, the worse it gets," I raised an eyebrow as a tear rolled down my cheek.

"It's already enough that you divorced Dad and he died soon after. Now, you're just going to replace him?"

"No, Rylie, it's not like that at all . . ." I heard her say as I bolted away from her bedroom, my face heated more than ever. I dropped off my backpack outside of my room, retrieving my phone from it before I rushed down the stairs to exit the house. I couldn't and wouldn't stay here for now. Everything was already too much for me to handle.

I couldn't fight back, either. Mom wouldn't tolerate and would go on and on about how she's not replacing Dad and all that bullshit. My brain can't take all that right now. My brain is still trying to process the whole Adrienne and Axel break up fiasco. How could an entire day have so much drama?

I needed to let all this off my chest, and I knew who to go to, so I settled towards his house, hoping that he was already back from city hall. He'd know what to say about this.

Where he resided wasn't too far from where I was, so I got there within several minutes. As I rung the doorbell, I crossed my fingers in hope that he'd be there. He had to be.

Ms. Greene answered the door with a shocked smile, the one someone would make when they got a magnificent surprise. "Rylie, what a surprise! What brings you here?" She questioned as she flashed a broad grin.

"Hi, I just came to . . . visit Elias for a bit. Is he here?" I questioned, crossing my fingers behind my back. My luck is normally rotten, so I just had to do that.

"He should be upstairs, so you can go check," Ms. Greene said as she let me in. "If you need any water or something eat, just let me know."

"Thank you," I muttered as I slipped my shoes off, placing them next to the door rug that had "Home Is Where The Heart Is" plastered across it in big letters. I walked up the flight of stairs and neared his bedroom, peering my head into it. He was nowhere to be seen. I went out into the hall to look around, but as soon as I heard a door open from the inside of the restroom, I knew he was there.

"Hey, Rylie. I didn't expect to see you here," Elias said, his cheeks reddening a bit. He was putting a clean shirt on, his entire chest revealed during the process. It was kind of hot and it did make me blush, as well. My mind began to wonder what he'd look like when he stepped out of the shower. That's probably where he just came from after all, judging from how he smelled. The mild aroma of cucumber body wash prickled my nose.

I shook the thought off. I can't believe thinking about what Elias Greene would look like walking out of the shower distracted my from my current issue. Was I actually that desperate? What a day.

23. Changes

ELIAS

"SO ARE YOU just going to keep staring at me, or what?" I questioned with a smirk, a chuckle escaping my mouth. "What brings you here?"

To my surprise, Rylie showed up my house, right when I finished taking a brief shower. She didn't say anything about coming over, but I didn't mind. I did have plans to work on an assignment for Physics, but that can wait. After all, she didn't seem to be okay. She had a broken look on her face. It was a defeated expression, one someone would make when they'd discover something unknown, yet significant to them.

Although, I shouldn't be making assumptions.

"Well, I just don't want to be at home right now. I hope you don't mind me staying here for a bit," Rylie murmured as she brushed her foot against the tan, carpet ground.

"I don't mind one bit. Let's go to my room," I gestured her to the second room down the hall—my bedroom. She made herself comfortable by laying down on my bed, while I sat down at the rim. I forgot to make my bed this morning and my room was an entire dump. Rylie didn't seem to mind, so far, though, so I questioned, "What's the problem?"

"It's my mom. The minute I got home, I was in for this unexpected surprise. It wasn't a good surprise," she groaned as she planted her hands over her eyes. Rylie began to explain how she found her mother in bed with a man, only to turn out that it was her boyfriend. According to her, her mom's been dating this man for a year.

She let out a long groan before being interrupted by a series of notification rings from her phone. "It's my mom wondering where I am," she shook her head as she typed in something before putting her phone away on my night stand. "I just can't believe she'd hide all this from me for a year. Imagine if she's trying to replace my dad..."

"I'm sure she isn't trying to do that. Your mom probably just wants to date," I assured her with the best reason I could come up with.

"Maybe, but that doesn't excuse the fact that she hid all this from me for nearly a year. A whole freaking year, Elias," she countered. It was a whole different side of Rylie. She was aggrivated, and I couldn't quite blame her for it. It must've been a lot to deal with all at once.

"It doesn't, but maybe she had her reason to do it. I'm sure she didn't do it to hurt you or anything," I managed to say.

"I don't know anymore," Rylie groaned as she dug her hands into her face. "This is just . . . too much."

I laid down next to her and sort of cupped my hand over hers for a few moments before letting go. "Look, everything will be alright, Rylie. It may be hard, but just take everything a step at a time. It'll take to get used to all these changes, take baby steps," I assured her.

"I guess you're right," she gave in. "Thanks for the words of encouragement."

"Anytime," I flashed a smile before staring at the ceiling. It was porcelain white and blank, like a fresh sheet of printer paper. My mind flew back to how crazy today turned out to be. Adrienne and Axel broke up, I finished the last touches of my painting so it could be judged for the art contest, and now this. How crazier could a day possibly get?

The possibilities are endless.

The room was hushed to the point where you could hear a pin drop to the ground. I didn't know what to bring up, like usual, and I assume that Rylie doesn't either. This is just another occasion of my brain malfunctioning to the point where I don't know what to say. I slouched up a bit, my elbow against the bed so my head could lean on my hand. Rylie was wearing a light grey sweater and black jeans with mix-matched socks, one with purple bunnies and the other with multiple-colored stripes. It was sort of cute.

"Nice socks, Rylie," I couldn't help but laugh. I wasn't making fun of her or anything. I've actually had worse times where I had mix-matched socks. Pretty much, every day.

"Yours are nicer," she cackled as she pointed to mine. One had a very unsatisfied Squidward plastered across the middle, while the other was maroon red and had the word "Tuesday" plastered over it, even if it was actually Monday. It seemed childish, but that's where the nostalgia comes from.

"They're both nice, although yours are way better by a landslide," I countered playfully as she nudged my shoulder.

"Ah, I give up already," she chuckled. "You're probably gonna come up with a million reasons for why mines are better. You win."

"You got that right," I teased as I looked into her mocha eyes. Before neither of us could say anything else, a recurring knock on the door sounded before whoever was there came in. It was my dad with a tray, two clear cups of water on top.

"Water, anyone?" He offered with a grin.

"Thanks, Dad," I got up from the never-ending comfort of my bed to retrieve both cups so Rylie wouldn't have to get up. She did end up getting up to take a couple of sips before saying thanking my dad for bring us water as she placed the half-empty cup on my night stand. I did the same.

"It's no problem," he said before he left, but peered back at me for a few moments with what seemed like a wink. "And Elias, don't cause a lot of trouble with your girlfriend up here and everything."

"Dad," I groaned as my hand met my forehead as he closed the door shut behind him, making a small clicking noise.

"He still thinks that we're . . ." Rylie chuckled as her index fingers lightly touched each other. "Together?"

"Yeah, but he also likes to do that to embarrass me," I added as I rolled my eyes playfully. "Typical parent move."

She nodded with a grin as we stared at each other, eye to eye. It made me feel butterflies flutter through my stomach freely. We were close to each other, literally inches apart. Definitely less than twelve, that's for sure. She cupped her hand over mine, just like I did earlier, but in contrast, she kept it there.

My heart tensed. The butterflies I felt kept on flying, however, this time I felt more. My mind trailed back to all the times Rylie and I did things together—whether if it were talking or watching a movie, it mattered to me. Those moments we shared were valuable like gold. They were firsts and I cherished every since second of each.

I like Rylie. It sounds cheesy, but I do. I want to show her, so I think it's time I face the music.

"Rylie, can I . . . kiss you?" I questioned hesitantly. "You know, you don't have to say yes." Instantly, regret boiled through my veins. What if this was all just a big mistake? What if she got mad and decided to leave. Her day was already too much and I didn't want to add more drama to it.

Okay, Elias, breathe. Focus on what's happening right now.

"You can," she chirped.

I practically did an cringe-worthy celebratory dance in my head, but no one could see it, so no one would care. I leaned in so my lips could hover over hers, the feeling igniting my entire body.

I pulled away in case she felt uncomfortable. But instead, she pulled back in to kiss me back. Her lush lips grazed over mine. She let out a soft moan before pulling away. I never wanted it to end, but soon, it did.

She inched away from me to the other side of my queen-sized bed. Regret began to boil through my veins, however as soon as she turned on my lamp at my night stand, the regret slowly began to vanish. The room was getting dark from the sun setting and all, so it did make sense to have a light on. Rylie scooted closer to me, this time closer than ever. I found my hand grazing across her upper back, but my heart sunk. Something hit me right at this moment.

"Rylie, if there's something I do that you don't like, just let me know," I assured her as I let go from touching her. "I'll stop right away, I promise."

"I'll keep that in mind," she mused as she combed a hand through my moisturized, brunette natural curls. "You're so sweet for that—and everything else. That's why I like you, Elias. It took me quite some time to figure it out, but I like you."

I paused for a second. My brain was doing a horrible job at processing every word that came out of her mouth, so I was speechless, barely managing to say anything in response. "I-I like you too, Rylie," I croaked as my hand sort of played with the sleeve of her sweater.

She smiled a bit at my response, her hand trailing down to my chin. Her thumb grazed over it lightly, like a cloud. Before anything else could be said or done, the loud ringing of Rylie's phone prickled my ears. It was the default Apple tone, so of course it was loud. Rylie extended her hand to reach the night stand to retrieve her phone, groaning at the caller ID.

"It's my mom," she sighed as she looked down towards my bed while drawing shapes through the sheets. "I should get going."

"Alright, then, see you tomorrow?" I offered.

"See you tomorrow," her voice mirrored mine as she leapt off of my bed.

Then, I offered to walk her out, but she insisted that it wasn't necessary. I didn't fight back, so I stayed in the presence of my bedroom. I laid down, my arms and legs spread out as if I were a young child making a snow angel in the snow. Today may have been crazy, and that was a fact, but for me, it ended off on a good note.

Who knew that kissing could feel so . . . great? I never wanted the moment to end, but there are still more to come, hopefully. The kiss felt sort of . . . arousing. It triggered a whole different feeling that I wanted to feel a lot more of. I definitely will be thinking about it for the rest of the evening, for sure. It was a first and I definitely didn't want to make it my last. Life can be shitty sometimes, but you have to admit that there are still some things to look forward to. This is a perfect example.

And I cherished it.

24. Sorting It Out

RYLIE

I REFUSED TO go in. I didn't want to. Not even the recurring, cool air of the wind tempted me to go inside the house. It was like something was holding me back. If I went inside, I'd have to face Mom. I didn't have the motivation to do so right now. For one, she'd probably be pissed that I ignored her call. For two, she may be mad that I decided to storm off. Should I have done that? Of course not, but my emotions earlier said otherwise.

I figured that it would be best to face the music and get over it afterwards, so I unlocked the door with my house key and walked in. I placed my shoes near the door, next to Cookie's cat bed. She was sleeping gracefully, so I was careful not to wake her up.

"I'm home," I croaked as I trudged through the foyer to the living room. From my view, Mom was in the kitchen, her eyes focused on the screen of her laptop as she ate what seemed like takeout. She's the one who made up the rule of no electronics being out during dinner, yet she was alternating between typing and eating noodles with a fork.

Her house, her rules, I guess.

"Rylie, you're back!" Her face brightened up with a relieved smile as she gently closed her laptop screen. "I was worried about you. How come you didn't answer my call?"

"I was on my way home, so my service was . . . bad," I blurted out. That was a lie. Definitely not the best one, but I didn't want her to think that I was ignoring her on purpose.

"Okay," she squinted at me, but sighed after. "Have a seat. I saved some takeout for you."

I slumped into the chair. There was a takeout compartment plate placed in a plastic bag, alongside napkins and a fork. When I opened it, there was half rice, half noodles, alongside bourbon chicken. They were all foods I particularly liked, so I couldn't help but wonder: Was she trying to bribe me into something?

Maybe I was just overthinking things.

The room was silent. Mom looked like she was about to say something, but she held it back. I took this as time for my mind to trail back to everything that's happened within the past hour. It was unbelievable and I wanted to think that I was dreaming, but in reality, I wasn't.

Elias kissed me.

In my head, I practically panicked. Not in a bad way, like I did earlier when Mom got caught with her not-so-secret boyfriend, but in a great way. In a way that was . . . dazed, shocked, and excited. A blush crept up my cheeks as I thought about it, even though my skin is as brown as chocolate, that didn't stop it. It just hid it.

Of course, my thoughts had to be interrupted by the noise of Mom cleared her throat.

"Rylie," she croaked as she looked me in the eye. "I can explain everything."

As I twirled my fork through my noodles, I raised an eyebrow. "I already know the entire story, Mom. What else is there to talk about it? You're just trying to replace Dad and you just had to hide it from me. I get it."

"No, that's not how it is, Rylie," Mom countered as she shook her head. "I may be dating someone else, but that doesn't mean I'm trying to replace your father." She continued with a sigh. "Your father is still your father, no matter what, but I want to date. The divorce left me feeling overwhelmed and lonely."

"Fine, but who even is the guy you're dating? You never even bothered to introduce me to him all this time," I argued as I poked my fork into my chicken. "You only told me his name."

"Well, Kaden is a great guy. He's super friendly and I think you'll like him," Mom admired as a blush crept up her cheek. Her voice sounded all gush y and I couldn't help but shake my head.

Don't get me wrong. I want my mom to be happy and all. She's already dealing with enough stress to keep a roof over both of our heads, but that doesn't excuse the fact that she hid the truth from me for nearly a year.

"Mom, why did you decide to hide this all from me for nearly a year? What made you think that it would be okay?" I questioned as I pushed away my food. All this conversation nauseated me to the point where my stomach began to churn.

"Rylie, I know I should've told you about all this sooner, however, I didn't know how I would," she sighed as she planted a hand over her forehead. "I didn't know how you'd react, but now I realize that hiding it more from you made everything much worse."

She shook her head lightly as she pushed away her plate. I guess I'm not the only one who feels weird about this conversation.

I couldn't say that it was okay. I couldn't say that hiding the fact the she hid the truth from me for almost a year was okay because it wasn't. I clenched my fists with disbelief as I shook my head, baffled on what to do.

So I didn't comment on it. "Can you at least introduce me to this guy sometime?" I asked.

"Of course. You're going to like him very much," Mom chirped. "How about sometime next week?"

I nodded as I grimaced back at my food. It was probably partially cold by now. Cold food isn't as great as warm food, in my opinion. However, I was starving, judging the amount of times by stomach grumbled unusually loudly, so I pulled the plate back to me to attempt to eat more. I still felt uneasy about the situation, but I need to set that aside. I can't let it get to me forever.

The rest of dinner was awkward. It wasn't that I wasn't used to it—it was just that the conversation we had about her new—or not-so-new boyfriend—was tense. It killed the vibe completely, kind of like bug spray when you kill a roach with it.

I managed the escape the awkward by going to my bedroom. I was working on notes for Physics while pondering about today, the good, the bad, and the in-between. My mind kept trailing back to the kiss. It was surreal and mind blowing.

I shared a kiss with Elias Greene.

I've never kissed anyone, so this was a first. It was better than it seemed before it all happened. The kiss wasn't that steamy, but it was still amazing. I decided to call Nora to tell her all about it. She ended up answering the phone in a heartbeat.

"Ry!" She gleamed as I could hear what seemed like a glass cup set down on a table. "What's up?"

"A lot," I slurred my voice. I told her everything—from catching my Mom with her boyfriend and going to Elias' house. Nora was supportive enough to assure me that she had a reason behind everything—but eh. I also informed her about Elias and I kissing.

"You guys kissed? That's crazy," Nora practically screamed into the phone, like an aunt finding out spectacular news.

"Yes, we did. It felt so good," I admired as I sunk into my desk chair.

"He totally likes you. Are you guys official, or . . . ?" She suggested. I could sense her winking behind the screen. I could just feel it.

"Not yet, from what it seems like," I clutched my fingers together.

"You two should get together. You and him are so cute together," Nora raved as I heard what seemed like pages flipping from a book or something.

I laughed at the thought. I didn't disagree. "Alright, I have to go now. Bye, Nora."

"Bye, and good night," she purred before ending the call.

How on Earth was I supposed to make things official? When would I do it? I had so many questions, but no answers, so I did what could've been the best decision possible: turn to Google. I opened a new tab on my laptop and typed in "how to make a relationship official". The first thing that popped up was a WikiHow article titled "How to Get in a Relationship".

I clicked the link eagerly. A picture of a couple holding hands as the first step popped up. I read over all the steps and tips within several minutes—mainly 'cause the article had three steps—multiple tips within each one. I scratched my head as my brain comprehended all the information that was entered into my brain. It was a lot, but I'm sure it'll be helpful.

The part I found most convenient was the article suggested the casual date. It wouldn't be too difficult to organize a time to hang out with him one on one. Asking him was the hard part. My mind began to trail different places. How would that work out? What if he refused?

Okay, maybe I'm overreacting, but that doesn't mean my point doesn't stand, still.

My laptop mouse hovered over the WikiHow's built-in search bar. I was desperate for ideas, so I looked up "best places to go on a date". One of the first options was titled, "5 Ways to Pick a Good Place to Go on Your First Date". It seemed relevant, so I clicked on it and scanned the article.

After I finished reading, I had a solid understanding on places to go. I exited off the WikiHow tab, feeling grateful that it exists. Sharing a meal together seemed like the best bet, other than taking a walk. We could easily do both in one day, but only if he wants to as well.

I think I'll ask Elias about it tomorrow. Life is short. Waiting for things to just come to you sometimes is more time consuming, so it's worth a shot.

***

By the time lunch period rolled around, I found myself walking with Nora, Cannon, and Elias to the lunchroom. I was contemplating on whether I should tell Elias now, or save it for later during last period. Nora and I discussed it earlier during homeroom a bit and she thinks I should go ahead and rip off the bandage. In other words, I should do it.

"Cannon," Nora nudged his shoulder. "I have some fabrics to show you, but their in my locker. Wanna go see them?"

That was the part Nora planned out just so I could ask him. It seemed like a great reason, so I don't see why Cannon would refuse.

"Oh, cool. Let's see them, then," Cannon approved.

"Awesome," Nora said as she practically grabbed Cannon by the arm to drag him in the opposite direction of the crowded corridor. She winked at me through the process as I exhaled a breath. Elias and I were alone. Not alone in the hallway, but alone where no one else would interrupt us.

"So it looks like it's just us heading down to the cafeteria?" Elias proclaimed as we swung around a corner.

"Yep," I nodded as I adjusted by backpack strap. "There's something I wanted to tell you, actually. Just me and you."

"What is it?" His eyes widened.

"I want to take things between you and I to the next step," I tried to face him, but found myself looking at my black, leather boots instead. My face heated as I took a deep breath. "Will you go out on a date with me?"

25. New Truths

ELIAS

"YOU WANT TO go out . . . on a date? With me?" I questioned, trying not to break out dancing with excitement right there in the hallway. "Of course."

I was smiling like an idiot on the outside, but in the inside, I was having a whole party. A date. I'm going out on a date with Rylie. I wasn't shocked, considering everything that happened yesterday, but that didn't stop me from being excited.

"Last night, I was thinking of places we could go," she suggested as we climbed down a mildly crowded stairwell, students here and there. "Do you have any suggestions?"

On our way to the lunchroom, we ended up discussing places we could go to for our date. It took quite some thinking, but we both agreed it would be nice to dine at a restaurant, specifically on the same day where the TCVA winners will be announced. If I win, dinner will be the perfect way to celebrate, but if not, that doesn't mean that dinner will be any less special.

For lunch, I ended up ordering a brown rice bowl with teriyaki chicken and vegetables alongside apple slices and water. Once both of our lunches were paid for, we trotted to our usual table. Surprisingly, Nora and Cannon were already there, mooning over a photo on Cannon's phone as if they were staring at a newborn baby.

I was too excited about the date that I could hardly manage to eat my food. By the time lunch period was over, I barely managed to get done with my rice bowl, even if I already ate the vegetables, apple slices, and drunk about half of my water. I felt butterflies flow freely in my stomach as I threw away my food. My brain still couldn't comprehend the fact that I will be going out on a date with Rylie.

Cannon, who seemed to notice how excited I was, could tell. "Why are you so excited, Eli?"

"Rylie asked me out on a date. A date," I sort of squealed like a crazy fangirl. An excited one, too.

"No way. That's crazy," Cannon's mouth spread open with shock. "When is it going to be? We need to discuss what you're going to wear, what you two are gonna do . . ."

"It's going to be on Saturday, the same day where the art contest winners will be announced," I raved as we steered our way around a mob of students. In between classes, there is no such thing as a clear path to walk through, specifically in a straight line. You always have to curve your way around people who decided it would be nice to create traffic and stand around in the middle of the halls.

That's Crews, for you.

"That's so exciting," Cannon cheered as we sauntered inside our next period. Within the time frame of class almost starting, I informed him about yesterday, specifically about the kiss. It made my stomach churn, but in a good way. Everything that happened was a first, and I definitely don't want it to be my last.

***

Two days later, a cloudy Thursday after school, Cannon agreed to lend me a ride home. I patiently waited at the exit that lead to the student parking lot for him, since I already had all the belongings I needed to head home. The problem with getting a ride from someone is simply waiting. You always have to be on someone else's time, not your own. That's how it is for me all the time, since I don't have a car. A lot of times, I can't even borrow my mom or dad's car because they take it back and forth to work and other places during the day.

I can't exactly say it's okay, because it isn't, however, I don't mind waiting in a time like this. As soon as I get home, I'll have to dig my head into some textbook and study. It'll have to be done sooner or later, but for now, I was slouched on a bench outside the student parking lot, right under the shade of the outdoor roof, sketching away a skyscraper in my sketchpad. Probably the third one I've used up this year. In my opinion, my sketchbooks are pages upon pages of random thoughts expressed on paper.

Endless thoughts expressed on paper, actually.

I took a moment to check the time on my phone. It was two-thirty five, around fifteen or so minutes after the school day ended. By now, the corridors were empty and the exterior exits weren't opening and shutting every second. Other than students who stayed for extracurricular activites and several teachers, there was hardly anyone left at school, except for students who were waiting on their rides home.

By now, Cannon should've been done with gathering all this things. Instead of shooting him a text to see where he was, I headed inside to get him, because chances are, he probably wouldn't answer anytime soon. I walked my way to the corridor where his locker was. It didn't take me long to get there because there weren't any students blocking the way. Sure, I passed a few janitors wiping windows with glass cleaner and cloth and a librarian wheeling a cart of books into and elevator, but it wasn't bad. They weren't all bunched up together, like a crowd.

To my surprise, he wasn't anywhere to be seen. I wasn't about to search the entire school for him, so I shot him a text, questioning where he was. I made a sharp U-turn to head down the nearest stairwell to go to the art room. The chances of him being there are slim, but it's worth a shot. Midway through the stairs, the steps of another person sauntering to the bottom like I was ringed my ears from behind me. My head swung back to see who it was.

Rylie was there, practically rushing her way down to me. Her shoulder-length natural twists swayed back and forth as she approached me, a shocked grin spread across her face. "I didn't expect to see you here, Elias. You're normally in the art room at this time," she took a heavy breath. "Are you heading home?"

"I am, but I'm looking for Cannon. He's giving me a ride. You?" I said as my thumb brushed on the smooth railing of the stairs.

"I'm going home, as well. I'm just waiting for Nora. We're supposed to go shopping or something," Rylie chirped as she dug her hands into the pocket of her hoodie. It was light grey and had Squidward plastered over it. I couldn't help but smile, since SpongeBob used to be one of my favorite television shows.

"I'm just really excited for our date, Rylie. I can't believe it'll be after tomorrow," I raved as we went through a set of double-doors. "I've been saving up and everything."

"Same here," her eyes met mine before her phone pinged. She took it out of her pocket to see what was up. "Nora is outside waiting for me. I have to go now."

"See you tomorrow," I said before she could leave, but I wrapped my arms around her to give her a brief hug. She returned the favor before pulling away, facing me with a slight smile before disappearing to the broad corridor that led to the student parking lot.

I smiled to myself as I hiked to the hallway with all the art and woodworking classes. I peeked my head through the doorway of Ms. Edwards' classroom, my eyes instantly widening. What my eyes were currently seeing was something I would never expect to see ever in my life.

Axel and Cannon were there at our usual table, Ms. Edwards nowhere to be seen. They were sitting on separate stools, Cannon's arms wrapped around Axel's body. Axel did the unthinkable by leaning his head on Cannon's shoulder.

"They wouldn't approve of this," Axel muttered as he sort of shook his head. "They just wouldn't."

"Everything will be okay . . . they'll eventually understand, hopefully," Cannon reassured him as he brushed his shaggy, raven black hair with his free hand.

Who is they? What were they talking about? Why are they cuddling with each other? I had so many questions, but I knew one thing: there was no way Axel was gay—or at least bi. Is he and Cannon together? There's no way, since Axel just broke up with Adrienne. The only way to get answers was to ask.

"Uh... What's going on?" I croaked as I cleared my throat. Both of their eyes widened with shock as Axel got up from Cannon, his hand cupped over his mouth.

"I— Elias," Axel muttered as he threw his backpack on his shoulder. "What are you doing here?"

"I was looking for Cannon," I replied briefly as I shot him a perplexed look. "You guys were cuddling. I don't mean to be nosy, but are you two..." I lightly made gestures with my fingers.

"We're not, Eli. We were just..." Cannon answered as his voice trailed off, "hugging. That's all."

I shrugged, satisfied enough with the answer as I neared our usual table. My mind still reflected off to everything I just saw and heard. All my questions still weren't answered. Maybe I don't need a response, but it'll keep me wondering for quite some time.

"I know this will sound weird, but what did you mean by they? What did you mean by a certain someone approving of . . . this," I questioned as I took a seat on a stool across from them.

"It's . . . it's a lot," Axel admitted as his voice trailed off, his eyes fixated on the table.

"You don't have to share," I assured him as I stared into his eyes. Serious and broken-looking, from view.

"I've been meaning to do this . . . for a while now," he confessed as he sighed heavily. "I'm bi. There's no other way to put it. Before Cannon knew it, Adrienne was the only person that knew, and that's shorty before we broke up," he shook his head. "My parents are extremely conservative. They wouldn't approve of, well, this."

"They'll have to learn to accept it all once you tell them," Cannon suggested.

"And that's the problem. They don't really . . . support this. I'm just tired of hiding all this from them, but one day, I'll have to break the news," Axel shook his head. "It's been invading my mind to the point where I decided to just . . . drop out of the art contest."

My expression was blank. I was shocked to learn new information about Axel. I had no clue that he was bi. He was good at hiding it, maybe because he was dating Adrienne all this time. All of this could've contributed to their breakup, but who knows?

What shocked me more was that all this was affecting him so badly to the point where he dropped out of TCVA. He looked forward to the contest so much. He could've won again this year possibly.

"It won't be easy, but I'm wishing you the best of luck, Axel. I truly am," I mustered a hopeful grin. It was the most honest smile I've exchanged with him since forever.

"Thank you," he returned the smile.

"I'm rooting for you, as well," Cannon joined in before glancing at his smartwatch. "Looks like we should get home now, Eli. I've kept you waiting long enough."

"You have, but it's all good," I nodded as I adjusted a strap of my backpack.

26. Revealed

RYLIE

MY ROOM WAS a complete mess. A mess that would take literally forever to clean up.

It was an unusually sunny, winter Saturday, a few pillow-like clouds dotted across the sky. I hadn't stepped outside yet, but judging from the leaves on the trees swaying back and forth from the view of my bedroom window, it's chilly. I, however, was warm by the comfort of my bed as Nora organized an entire outfit for me to wear for later.

Good thing we went shopping the other day for clothes. Nora basically picked them all out for me (with my approval, of course). She was convinced that they had variety, unlike all the clothes in my closet. She isn't wrong, though. All I have is hoodies, sweaters, leggings, sweatpants, and jeans. Since I'm going out on a date, it does make sense that I at least wear something a little different from my style.

"Ta-da! How about this?" Nora gleamed as she gestured to the beige cami dress she was holding up, alongside a white sweater to go under it.

"It's nice, I guess" I said with acknowledgement. Sure, a cami dress isn't exactly something I'd wear on a normal basis, but it did look nice. It was a simple dress, at least, rather than being an unnecessarily poofy ball gown.

"I'm glad. Go put it on," she beamed as she handed everything to me with care. I gathered the dress into my arms and settled towards the bathroom. I showered around thirty minutes ago, before Nora got here, so I was already freshened up. I made sure to shave my legs and unravel my curls, as well.

After I got my clothes on, I tossed the sweater and sweatpants I was wearing before into the laundry hamper in the corner. When I looked into the mirror, I realized that I looked presentable. I didn't want to put on any make-up or anything, so before I abandoned the bedroom, I sprayed perfume all over me, the sugary aroma prickling my nose.

"You look so beautiful, Rylie," Nora admired as her hands clasped together. "As always."

"Thank you, Nora," I said as I grabbed my small, golden yellow purse (filled with many toiletries and my phone) and swung it on my shoulder. "Let's go."

Even though I still had the date to go to, it was still early. I agreed to go to Elias' award ceremony for his art contest. I didn't mind at all. It would be great if he won because I know it means a lot to him, since he wants to show his parents that he has potential to become a successful artist. I'm in for it all the way.

I already told Mom about going out to the ceremony and date before she headed out to work this morning, so I was good to go. Since she doesn't normally work on Saturdays, part of me was convinced that she was actually hanging out with that boyfriend of hers, but it doesn't matter. What matters is the fact that she still hasn't organized an occasion for me to properly meet him. It's possible that she's waiting for winter break, but I shook my head. Today is a big day and

I shouldn't be thinking about this. I have two things to look forward to, so I should focus on them.

As I fastened my seat belt, I took a breath, hoping that I wasn't late. I took my phone out of my purse to check the time. It was five twenty-one, so the ceremony would start in about nine minutes. Yep, I'm running late. It'll take a few minutes to get to the arena, seven at most, so I may be on a good note.

The ride to the arena felt long. Nora spent the entire time raving about her Christmas wish list and accessories she's designed lately as I was slumped in my chair, tired of waiting. When we pulled up at the arena, excitement boiled through my veins. I could hardly contain it all.

"Thanks for the ride," I acknowledged as I stepped out of the car with one foot, the other following.

"No problem. Make sure you tell me everything," Nora prompted with a grin.

I nodded as I made a mental note to do so. The arena was tall and broad, a few people swarming into the establishment. When I got inside, I saw a chalkboard on an easel that read, "The Crews City

Visual Arts Contest in Ballroom Five" with an arrow pointing to the right. I saw a few people heading in the same direction I was, so I didn't feel lost. When I reached the ballroom, I instantly saw a stage and dozens of seats with people situating themselves.

The ballroom was a little smaller than an average ballroom, but it was big enough to fit just about everyone who was in the room. The ceiling was tall and the room was broad. At the back, there was a table with a water dispenser and cups, alongside fresh-brewed coffee, the nutty smell flowing throughout the room.

I squinted at the mobs of people all around the room in an attempt to locate Elias. From what it looked like, he was nowhere to be seen. I got ready to take out my phone and text him, but before I could do so, I felt a light tap creep up my shoulder. My head swung around with shock, only to smile later at who it was.

"Elias! I didn't think I'd find you in all these people," I remarked as I planted my hands over my hips. Elias was dressed nicely with a formal, sapphire blue white shirt, black pants, and dress shoes to match. This was the fanciest I've seen him dressed, and my mouth couldn't help but drop open. "You look handsome," I admired.

"And you look gorgeous, like usual," he shot back in a friendly manner. My face couldn't help but heat up at his cheesy response. "I saved us seats up front."

I followed him through mobs of socializing people to our seats in the second row, right at the end of the aisle, so we didn't have to walk through people's feet. There's nothing as weird as walking through people's feet and constantly saying "excuse me" and "sorry" at an important event. Once we were situated, I looked up to Elias, whose face had a stone-like expression.

"You look nervous," I said as I extended my arm so my hand could lightly meet his. "Don't worry, I believe in you."

"I don't know. I just feel so doubtful about all this," he sighed.

"That's normal, but don't let it take over your mind. I'm rooting for you," I assured him. I wanted to lean on his shoulder, but then I realized that it could've been considered PDA. I wasn't completely sure if Elias wanted it in front of so many people who probably weren't watching. I never asked, but I'm sure he wouldn't mind.

He cupped his hand over mine and brushed it as a middle-aged man held the microphone from the stage, the microphone creating a high-pitched squeak that not even Ariana Grande could hit. "Ladies and gentlemen, the school district and I would like to welcome you all to the Crews City Visual Art Contest, dedicated to showing the creativity in young adults," the man, who apparently was the assistant superintendent or whatnot announced as everyone fell into their places. "Thank you all for showing up at this fine evening to support."

A roar of cheers and claps erupted within an instant, and lasted a couple of moments before the announcer handed the microphone over to a woman, who presumably appeared to be one of the judges for the art contest. "Ladies and gentlemen, thank you for coming out. I am one of the judges for the contest and will now announce the top three winners. Please come to the stage when you hear your name," the woman announced with a broad grin. "Even if your name doesn't get announced, your art will be returned to you afterwards. Prizes will be given, as well."

Goosebumps crawled up my skin as we all awaited the announcement of the top three winners. Elias appeared even more nervous as he bit his lip. Everyone else cheered and demanded to hear the winners.

"Our third place winner for this year is . . . Lorna Verrett," the judge cheered as she looked at a card. I had no clue who that was, but I began clapping slowly. One of the other judges removed a blanket that covered her painting, which was on an easel. Lorna took her place to the stage, her smile broad as she waved to the cheering crowd.

"Our second place winner for this year is . . . Elias Greene," the judge continued. Another judge uncovered his painting as he headed towards the stage, flashing me a relieved smile before heading off. I clapped as hard as ever, my hands reddening moments later. It was worth it.

"And our first place winner for this year is . . . Grayson Towler. Congratulations to all winners!" The judge concluded. "Thank you everyone for your participation and commitment." The room was filled with hollers, cheers, and rounds of applause for all three winners. Grayson gave a speech about how he was thankful for winning first place before the ceremony ended. I joined Elias at the stage, who was speaking with the judge.

I know how much he initially wanted first place. Second place is still good, but I don't think it'll offer the same prizes as first place. "Great job, Elias," I remarked as I stood next to him.

"Thank you," he acknowledged with a hopeful smile.

"You truly did a great job, Elias. We were pondering between Grayson's and your artwork between first and second place, but we'd still like to offer you the same prizes that you can get in first place," the judge remarked as she adjusted the rim of her eyeglasses.

"Really?" Elias' mouth dropped open with shock.

"Yes, but not only that. We'd also like to present your artwork in the Crews Museum of Modern Art. Us judges liked it very much," the judge offered with a grin. "Only if you want, of course."

"I'd love it. Thank you so much for the offer," Elias clasped his hands together.

"Great. We'll have your scholarship to Laurier ready for you, and your cash prize and summer tickets to Italy ready for you sometime in the next few weeks or so," the judge smiled.

"Thanks, again," Elias acknowledged. The judge nodded before sauntering towards Lorna, who was taking pictures with her family. Elias turned to me and reached out for a hug. "Thank you for encouraging me, Rylie. Should we head out to the restaurant now? I have my dad's car waiting outside."

"Definitely," I said as we made our way down the stage to abandon the room.

***

When we got to the restaurant, which was a few minutes away from the arena, Elias confirmed his reservations and the waitress escorted us to a table, not too far from the door. There were a few couples and families at tables nearby, but overall, the restaurant wasn't too busy. It was nicely decorated with modern decorations plastered on the beige walls.

I ended up ordering a chicken egg roll with various steamed vegetables to the side. It was simple, but it was a start. I decided to flip the switch and start the conversation instead, because usually, I don't. "Aren't you excited? You won all those cool prizes," I raved as I poked my fork through a piece of broccoli. "What do you plan on doing with them?"

"I'll probably end up saving the prize money for art supplies and things for the Italy trip, however the tickets to Italy . . ." Elias pondered as he placed his finger on the tip of his chin. "Since it's two tickets . . . do you want to go to Italy with me?"

Italy. The real Italy. I've never been to Italy before, but it sounds awesome. Eating actual pizza, taking dozens of pictures in front of the Leaning Tower of Pisa, touring through Venice—it all sounds amazing. It also sounds highly unbelievable since tickets would be highly expensive and I'd probably never be able to afford tickets on my own.

"Really? You want me to go with you?" I said, my mouth wide open with disbelief.

"Yeah . . . unless there's a problem with that," Elias' voice trailed off.

"There's no problem at all. I'd love to go to Italy with you," I raved before taking a sip of water.

"I'm looking forward to it, Rylie," he smiled as he adjusted his tie. "I feel like I've known you for the longest time, even if we've only known each other for . . ." he reflected as he counted on his fingers with his other hand. "Four months."

"Same here, and now that I think about it, I technically first saw you in art class on the first day of school," I added as I squinted my eyes.

Remembering that day made goosebumps crawl across my skin. I remember dreading that day completely, wanting to isolate myself from everyone. Now look at where I am. I guess you can say that my life took a completely different route that I originally wanted to go on.

And I don't regret it all.

"Time flies by fast," Elias winked before poking his fork through the last bits of his salad. At this point, we were halfway done through firsts and moving onto seconds.

I nodded in agreement at his response and sawed my knife through my eggroll. If it weren't for this date, I would've been a bit more messy and eaten it with my hands. Let's be real, through—I don't need Elias to have a bad impression of me actually eating so sloppily, especially on our first date. Then again, he seems like the guy who wouldn't care, but who knows.

We got through dinner and desserts maybe thirty or so minutes later. It wasn't awkwardly silent, fortunately. We had an engaging conversation about random things about us, such as what we like doing, our goals, and everything in between. It was rather interesting.

I was stuffed from the meal to the point where I could hardly move. It's probably the best dinner I've had since Thanksgiving break.

When it was time for us to pay, Elias handed our waitress from earlier his debit card so it could be processed for our payment. I insisted on paying as well, but Elias insisted that he should've done it instead. I didn't counter his argument, but we were both in for a surprise when the waitress came back.

"Sir, I swiped your card in, but it declined," the waitress reasoned.

"In that case, I don't have enough money . . ." he grimaced as he dug his hands into his pockets. "Can you put all the money I have on the card into the bill and pay the rest in cash," he glanced at the receipt.

"Absolutely," the waitress nodded. I began to look through my purse to see if I had any extra dollars laying around. I happened to have a few various bills that added to nine dollars.

"You can use this," I stacked the money on the palm of my hand to hand it to the waitress.

"Thank you, miss. It should be enough," the waitress proclaimed before sauntering away.

"Rylie, you didn't have to do that," Elias reasoned as he placed a ten dollar bill and a few coins onto the table. "I had enough."

"It's okay. You paid for the entire bill, so it only makes sense if I pitch in," I shrugged with a wink.

"You have a point," Elias mused as he placed the money at the side of the table for the tip. At that moment, the waitress came back with Elias' card and we prepared to leave the restaurant to head home. "After you, miss," he smirked as he held the door open.

"Thank you," I acknowledged. As we got settled in his dad's Toyota SUV, I snuck him a kiss on his cheek to thank him for everything. He returned the favor by kissing me back, but this time, on the lips, instead. The feeling of his soft lips coming into contact with mine made me feel like I was on cloud nine.

The kiss only lasted a few moments, but it felt like forever. I chuckled to myself lightly, pondering how amazing the day turned out to be. I was looking forward to more days like this. More days where I get to hang out with Elias and such.

His fingers laced around mine. We were still in the parking lot, the sky was darkening, but that didn't stop us. "I want to get to know you more, Rylie," he said as he looked me into the eye. He was serious. "Will you . . ."

"Go out with you? Of course!" I blurted, my voice a little raspy. Is it possible for a day to get any better than this?

"I'm glad to hear it," he pecked a kiss over my cheek. He kept his hand over mine. I could tell he didn't want to take it off from there, but he eventually did when he pulled out of the parking lot. He asked me for directions of where my house is, and I prepared to tell him a tale of lefts and rights. I didn't mind, though. I like Elias, and I wouldn't get tired of talking to him anytime soon.

27. New Faces

RYLIE

I SMILED LIKE an idiot as I bolted through the doors of home. Everything felt so magical. Today was an amazing day and I was looking forward to many more days like this. My mom, who was in the living room while on her phone, could tell.

"You seem a little happier than usual," Mom raised an eyebrow as she turned away from her phone, gesturing to me to take a seat next to her. "What's going on?"

"You know what's going on," I began as I sat down. "I went on a little date. It was nice."

"Oh, really? Did he confess his love to you?" Mom persisted.

"He did . . ." I said as I clutched my fingers.

"Nice, but like I said, don't grow up too fast. I don't need any surprises coming from you anytime soon," Mom reminded sternly.

"I know, I know," I nagged, my brain automatically triggered. I knew exactly what she was talking about when she said "surprises". Did she actually think I'd start doing that so soon? It's barely been even thirty minutes since we officially started dating, however, Mom is just looking out for me, as any mother should.

The room grew quiet again. Mom's phone pinged, tempting her to check what notification was on it. Her eyes lit up as she turned to me. "Remember when I said that I would arrange a time for you to properly meet Kaden?"

"Yeah . . ." My voice trailed off, an eyebrow cocked. "Why?"

"It's because tomorrow, he's inviting us over for dinner at his place," Mom chirped. My mood was the complete opposite.

"He's probably going to order food and have us eat it or something," I insisted with a disapproving sigh. "Do we have to go tomorrow, though?"

"Yes, we have to," she cooed, her voice sounding as if I was a baby and she was putting me to sleep. She planted a hand on my shoulder. "Please just give him a chance. He's a really nice guy."

"Sure, whatever," I looked away as I crossed my arms. I still wasn't over catching Mom with her little boyfriend. Everything was a complete surprise—definitely not the good ones everyone decides to keep you from on your birthday.

I still didn't understand it. Is Kaden actually a nice guy like Mom continuously claims him to be, or is he not? Until then, all I have is to think about how dinner would turn out to be.

***

We were at an apartment complex in town the next evening, right near school, too. The apartment complex itself was modern-looking and looked as if it were a few years old. The exterior is painted various shades of brown on the outside. The inside, however, wasn't how I envisioned it to look like. The floors were tile, not the old store-like tile, but a new kind of tile that you'd see in one of those home shows where they transform an old house into something completely new.

Is this seriously where this Kaden guy lives?

As we unboarded the elevator, goosebumps began to crawl all over my skin, like ants. The fact that I'm wearing an entire sweater (a nice one my mom forced me to wear) did no justice. Fear rushed through my veins, not knowing what to expect or what was about to happen. It's safe to say that Mom's little boyfriend is a complete stranger. The time we met . . . didn't count.

"Madeline! It's so nice that you made it," Kaden cheered as the door of his apartment swung open. "You too, Rylie." He extended his arm so his hand could meet mine.

I decided to not be polite, so I shook his hand. His hands were warm and sort of soft. At least they weren't cold, because cold hands just give a whole different feeling, the one that gives you shivers.

The apartment complex was simple. It wasn't all decorated and all. Everything seemed kind of bland, other than the photos hung up on the wall near the fireplace. I took a closer look at the frames, an eyebrow raised. None of the people in the photo looked familiar.

The photos consisted of a few people, four maximum, and no one looked like him in particular. Maybe they had younger versions of him. Some of the pictures looked sort of old, judging the poor quality of them. Who would've known?

The aroma of food floating into the living room from the kitchen prickled my nose. That's when Kaden decided to clasp his hands together and say, "The food is ready now, so shall we get eating?"

"Yes, but I need to wash my hands first," Mom said as she placed her purse on the light brown sofa. "I'll leave that time for you to talk a little." She wandered down the hall, only to disappear within a trace to a room. Specifically, the bathroom. Is Mom actually going to throw me under the bus like that? I don't want to be alone with him.

Only Kaden and I remained in the room. He gestured to me to follow him to the kitchen with a genuine smile. I expected to see pizza boxes or takeout meals on the table, but no. There were various bowls and plates filled with home-cooked foods. My mouth dropped open with shock as he pushed a seat out for me so I could sit down. I didn't expect to see a home-cooked meal. Really, I didn't expect to see much. Did he actually cook all this?

I still couldn't believe it. Not one bit.

The silence in the room was undeniably awkward. I know that I'm not the one who starts conversations, but I'm not pitching in this time. He probably took a hint, so he cleared his throat, "The last time we met was . . . shocking, but it's really nice to meet you, Rylie," he nodded his head as he pulled out a fruit punch from the refrigerator, kicking the door shut behind him. "Your mom told me all about you."

"I see. S-So you're actually her boyfriend?" I cocked an eyebrow. "Next thing you know, you two will get married and you'll become my new dad or something. I just know it."

Kaden stared down at the scarlet red tablecloth plastered across the table as he set the juice down, dazed. I cupped my hand over my mouth, dazed as well. What the fuck did I just say out loud to him?

"You don't have to worry about that anytime soon," he cooed, not seeming offended in any type of way. "I love your mother and all, but I want to wait a little while," he sort of whispered. "You don't have to worry about calling me "dad" or anything. Regardless of what you call me, it doesn't matter."

Good. I just met this guy. Calling him "dad" would be hella weird. Not to mention that I'm not intending on calling him my dad, anyway. Right at that moment, Mom appeared, shaking excess water off her hands.

"I'm back. Did you two have a good talk?" Mom cheered as she shot a convincing look at me. Obviously, she did this all on purpose.

"Yeah . . . we did," Kaden's voice trailed off as he pushed the chair Mom will be sitting in from the table so she could sit down. She snuck him a kiss on the cheek before she sat down, which made me cringe. I shook my head as my eyes focused on the table, not wanting to look up for the rest of the evening. To my bad luck, I wasn't able to.

Kaden said grace before we dug into the meal. It was fried rice alongside fried chicken. To my surprise, it had a zesty taste, the kind that made you want to eat more until you were stuffed. This made me wonder even more if Kaden actually made this.

Soon, to my luck, I'd get answers.

"Kaden, this food is amazing," Mom admired after swallowing a mouthful of fried rice. "You made this yourself? That's phenomenal."

"Yeah, I made it all for you and Rylie," he nodded as he popped open the bottle of fruit punch. "Juice, anyone?"

My mom agreed to have some, but I didn't, mainly because I was too drenched in my thoughts. Everything felt so unbelievable. Little did I know that those thoughts would carry throughout the rest of the evening.

When we were finished with dinner, Kaden agreed to let us stay, but Mom insisted that it was getting late. I was thankful that we'd soon be heading back to the comfort of our small, comfortable home. Kaden wished us a good night and kissed Mom—right on the lips—before we left. I couldn't help but cringe more at what I just saw.

"Now do you see that Kaden is a nice guy?" Mom smiled a little too broadly as we boarded her car.

"I guess," I muttered through gritted teeth as I fastened my seat belt.

"Come on, Rylie. Please be a little more open-minded about this," Mom sighed as she pulled the car out of the parking lot. "I'm not asking you to like my boyfriend. All I'm asking from you is to give him a chance."

I exhaled deeply, but said in response, "Fine."

Maybe I underestimated Kaden a bit, but one thing hasn't changed: I still don't like him.

***

When we got home, I changed into my mix-matched pajamas and lounged on my bed. Today was too much for my liking, but it made me realize that I hadn't really talked to Elias today, so I went through my contacts to call him. Not to tell him about my day, but to just talk.

He answered within the fourth ring, his voice ecstatic. "Rylie! What's up?"

"Not much," I shrugged as I dug my head into my pillow. "What's with you? Did you tell your parents about the prizes you won?"

"Not yet. I'm waiting for it to come in the mail so I can directly surprise them," he informed with a chuckle. "You know, to make it seem like I'm not playing a joke or anything."

"Makes sense," I nodded, even though he couldn't see me nod.

In the background, I could vaguely hear the noises of something falling, like a pot. He most definitely noticed it since he was there, so he addressed it. "Sorry about all the noise," he apologized with a nervous laugh. "I somehow pushed an entire cap of a pot off the counter top while trying to get a glass of water. It was so embarrassing."

"I can imagine, but we've all done something embarrassing once in a while, right?" I assured him with a chuckle. "It's what makes people people."

"You have a point," Elias replied as I could hear the noise of a door shutting close through the phone. "You know, I still can't believe yesterday. I could hardly sleep last night because of it. We're together."

"Yeah, I'm still trying to let it all sink in," I shifted to stare at the ceiling. Right then, my phone pinged. I looked up at the status bar on top, only for my mouth to drop open. My phone is at five percent. There was a feeling in my mind that tempted me to talk with Elias a lot more, but would that last with barely five percent left on my phone? Nope, it won't.

I could get my charger, but I'm sure it's stuffed away in my purse, which is hanging on the doorknob of my room. I wanted to get up to get it, but something was holding me back. I didn't have the motivation to, but I forced myself to get up and get my charger.

Everything fell silent on the phone. In the background, I could hear what seemed to be water gushing out of a tap. He must've been washing his hands or something, so I sighed, "My phone is about to die," I reasoned. "I need to let it charge, so talk to you tomorrow?"

"Definitely," he chirped. "Good night, Rylie."

"Good night, Elias," I cooed before I ended the call.

I plugged in my charger to the wall so I could charge my phone. In the meantime, I lifted a book off my nightstand and started reading from the first page, mainly to let my mind wander to many places. I couldn't help but think of how today turned out. It was a flop and I still couldn't refuse one idea.

I still didn't like Kaden.

28. Accomplishments

ELIAS

AROUND TWO WEEKS later, I found myself in the theatre during lunch period, procrastinating between sketching away and trying to study for final exams that would take place this week. It's ideal to set aside sketching, but let's be real, studying is tedious. Studying is something I just want to avoid under all costs, but does it look like I have much of a choice?

Nope, I don't.

Cannon, Nora, Rylie, and I were all situated together, all drenched in our separate conversations, definitely ignoring loud noises of the stage crew setting up props for one of their opening night. Cannon kept teasing me about me dating Rylie, right in front of her, too. I couldn't say that I'm surprised because I'm not. It's like he's the 2.0 version of my dad, but somewhat worse.

"It's been like, two weeks, since you two started dating," Cannon started after taking a bite of an apple. "How has it been so far?"

"It's been nice. Everything still feels like a dream, though," I remarked as I stared at Rylie, eye-to-eye. She nodded in agreement.

"Did you two . . ." he started to make light gestures with his two index fingers. I already could tell what it was, which caused my cheek to boil.

"No, we literally just started dating . . ." I snapped as I nudged his arms with a smirk.

"You sure?" Nora jumped in as she smiled at Rylie innocently.

"No way!" Rylie dug her hands into her face.

Neither of us were lying. It had only been two weeks since we started dating, so really, we didn't start fooling around. Well, not yet, at least. I'm not sure if we're ready yet. Let alone, if I'm ready yet. Either way, it's okay. There's no rush at all.

My mind wandered to the art ceremony that also took place two weeks ago. Winning second place, but still gaining all the prizes plus getting my art in the Crews City Museum of Modern Arts is spectacular. My other prizes still didn't come in the mail yet, but if I'm lucky enough, they may show up today.

Okay, maybe I'm just getting my hopes up, but still. Either way, I can't wait to tell my parents about it. I'll finally be able to not only make them proud, but to show them that I can pursue a decent career in art in the future, alongside another job. The exhibit will be the nicest proof. There's no way that my parents will be disappointed by that.

All I have to do is have hope.

***

"My fingers are crossed," Rylie chirped as she stood behind me, an assuring look plastered on her face.

"Mine are, as well," I took a breath as my hand grasped on the handle of the mailbox. School let out and Rylie and I decided to walk home. She insisted that we should start preparing for final exams, which are much closer than we think. You can say that it'll be like a study date and I'm actually stoked about studying for once.

Before we can even start studying, I still have to check the mail to see if my prizes were there. I peered into the mailbox, only to see that one envelope laid there. I foiled it out of the tight space it was in and read the name of the recipient.

It was me.

This only meant one thing: This has to be my prizes. I wanted to jump and dance all around, but that would be embarrassing. I'm not a good dancer and Rylie would see that. I didn't want to send that kind of message, so I remained still.

"The prizes are here," I held the envelope in my arms as if I was holding onto a newborn baby. "Let's go inside."

"That's awesome, Elias," she patted on my shoulder with a proud grin. "Will you tell your parents about it now?"

"Yeah, but we do have to study . . ." I reasoned as I reached into my pocket for my house key.

"That can wait," she let out a laugh as I unlocked the door. We both slipped off our shoes as soon as we got inside and got greeted by my parents soon after. They were excited to see Rylie with me and offered her food and drinks.

"Rylie, what brings you here? We didn't expect you to come here today," Mom cooed as she handed Rylie a glass of water. We were both situated on the couch, trying not to be so . . . PDA in front of my parents. They know that we're together, but I don't want to act like this in front of my parents, considering that my dad will make up corny jokes about it. Not that I don't mind, but it'll be cringeworthy.

"Elias and I were planning on studying for finals together," Rylie replied, which caused both of my parents to nod in approval. "However, Elias does have something to show you first."

Yep, I was thrown under the bus just like that. Was it worth it? Completely. I opened the letter as neatly as I could, loose pieces of the envelope flying everywhere. I pulled the letter out, as well as the check that contained my cash prize in it.

My eyes mooned over the letter, skimming over the words to see the information about the scholarship as well as the exhibit, which will be featured in the museum in a few months. It will take time, but every day will be worth it.

"I won second place in the art contest," I finally announced.

"Is it that art contest you were talking about once?" Mom questioned, her eyes gleaming.

"Yep," I nodded as I handed her the letter and checked so she could see for herself. Dad looked over her shoulder so she could see as well. "Turns out I won an art scholarship to Laurier, two tickets to Italy, a cash prize, and an art exhibit in the museum."

"No way. Ain't no way," Dad stumbled on his words as he peered closer at the check in Mom's hands. "Good job, son. I'm really, really proud of you."

"Me too. I mean, all these sound wonderful," Mom admired as she combed her hand through my curls.

"Is it . . . wonderful enough to make you believe that I do have potential to become an artist? Or at least have it as a second job?" My pitch went a little too high to the point where my voice painfully cracked, which caused Rylie to snicker a little.

Mom looked up to Dad, who nodded. "Yes, I think so. We're really proud of you, kiddo."

She handed me all the contents from the envelope back to me and I handed it to Rylie so she could take a look. Instead, she hugged me tightly. So much for not being PDA in front of my parents. However, I didn't care. I finally proved to my parents that I have potential to become an artist. It may have taken a long time, but it was a hundred percent worth it.

"Should we get studying now?" she suggested as she let go from me.

"Yeah, we should," I leapt off of the couch so I could help her up. As we made our way up the stairs, Mom reminded us if we should let her know if we needed anything and Dad shot me a wink. A wink that meant to not get into trouble or anything.

I just shook my head. Again, it's only been two weeks.

When we got to my room, a feeling hit me. The same feeling that tells you that you should've done something, but you didn't. My room was a mess yet again. I mean, there is only a few clothes and papers over the floor, but that still counts as messy. I kicked a dirty shirt under my bed before taking a seat at the rim.

"Ugh, I just wish we didn't have to have final exams," Rylie groaned as she took out a spiral notebook from her backpack. "Too much pressure."

"If only it wasn't mandatory," I flipped into my notebook. "Imagine if it wasn't." Let's be real—that'll never happen, but it would be cool if it did.

"That would be nice, for once," Rylie hummed as she took out a highlighter to go over her notes. Even if it's only been two weeks, I've learned a lot more about her. She's not a fan of large family gatherings, homework, or dresses. She also gave me an update on what's happening at home—which is mainly about her mom's boyfriend.

I didn't mind talking about it, although I still think that she shouldn't be stressing about it too much. I just don't want her to stress too much about everything. School alone is already stressful enough as the semester comes to an end.

Speaking of the semester coming to an end, we both looked over our notes and sort of quizzed ourselves over things we've learned throughout the semester. It was sort of productive, but we did go off-track a couple of times.

"Do you have any resolutions for the new year coming soon? Or even next semester?" Rylie questioned as she closed her neon yellow highlighter, the cap making a clicking noise.

"Well, other than being a little more productive in studying," I reasoned as I planted a finger on my chin, "I want to spend more time with you. School will be busy as always, but I still want to make time for you. Sometimes, everything feels so empty . . . but you were the highlight of my entire school year."

At this point, we were so close to each other that I could smell her scent, which was a mix of cocoa butter and the sugary aroma of lavender. I could feel her warmth as she breathed. Before I could even say anything else, she quickly leaned forward, lips touching mine. I grazed my thumb over her cheek tenderly as I kissed back, her hot breath prickling my neck.

It was a feeling like no other. It was soft, tender, and sweet—the feeling that made you want more. Rylie tugged on the sleeve of my navy blue sweater as she let go of the kiss. It all felt different, maybe because we were in a bed, but I quickly shook off the thought. The room was unusually quiet and we could both sense it obviously, so

Rylie questioned, "When you were little, before you even wanted to become an artist, what did you want to be?"

I shook my head with a chuckle, "A superhero." It was true. All the cartoons I watched when I was younger made me believe that being a superhero was an actual job. Television made it look so impressive, more impressive than any other job. Soon after, I discovered my passion for art and didn't think about being a superhero again.

Well, until now.

"A superhero," her chuckle echoed mine. "That's interesting."

"Yeah, so that technically means I've only ever wanted to be two things," I counted on my fingers to confirm it. "What about you?"

"When I was younger, I wanted to be a detective because I liked reading the Nancy Drew series . . . and she was a detective," she snorted. "But as I grew older, I wanted to be something in the psychology field, like a therapist or something. For some reason, I think it would suit me fine."

"I remember talking about this once. You still haven't figured out what exactly you want to be?" I questioned.

"Nope," Rylie hummed as she changed her position on the bed. She was now laying down on her back, while I was still on my side. "I'll figure it out soon."

"I know you will," I assured her. Rylie nodded as she went back to staring at the spotless, white ceiling. That's when I realized that we'd gotten extremely sidetracked from studying. I couldn't say I was surprised, but the whole point of this was to study for finals. I didn't mind that we didn't do what was originally planned, though. Sometimes, that's just how life is.

29. Sweet Like Candy

RYLIE

AS SOON AS I walked through the door, I wanted to walk back out. It was an afternoon after school, and frankly, I wanted to go back. Kaden was on the couch, all in a casual tracksuit as Mom was nowhere to be seen. I started to believe that I walked into the wrong house at the wrong time.

But no, I walked into the right house, unfortunately.

"Hey, Rylie. It's nice to see you," Kaden smiled with a wave.

I didn't want to sound rude, so I muttered. "Hi... what are you doing here? Where's my mom?"

"She went upstairs to grab something," he informed me briefly as I sauntered to the kitchen to grab some Cheetos out of the pantry. "How was your day at school?"

"It was okay, I guess," I resisted the urge to roll my eyes. Part of me knew for sure that he was pretending to be nice. I could see it in his face. Why did my mom have to date this random guy I barely knew anything about? Why did this guy have to come in and ruin everything?

There was no way I can easily hand over my trust to this guy. Who knows? He could just be pretending to be friendly just so he can hurt Mom later. It may sound delusional, but anything is possible. Anything.

Just then, Mom walked through the room, dressed in denim blue jeans and a white T-shirt to match. Thank the Lord I wouldn't have to spend another moment with her boyfriend alone. "Hey, Rylie. You're home early," she chirped.

I shrugged before biting into a cheeto, the thick, orange dust absorbing onto my fingers. I licked the dust off without hesitation. It may have been gross to do, especially in front of Mom's boyfriend, but I didn't really care.

"I have to get back to the office now. I'll call you as soon as I get there, Mads," Kaden cleared his throat as he got up.

"Alright then, have a safe drive," Mom beamed before planting her lips over his cheek. "I'll be at the office tomorrow morning 'till five. Will you be there then?"

"Yep, I will. See you then," Kaden said before his lips met hers. "Bye, Rylie."

I cringed at everything. I cringed at Mom's new nickname, replacing her perfectly fine first name, Madeline. I cringed at the kiss and the conversation. It made me nauseous to the point where I balled the Cheetos up and didn't even bother to lick off the excess Cheeto dust.

I watched Mom escort Kaden down the hall to the front door, where the kissed once more before he went out the door. I shook my head in disbelief as she came back to the living room, taking a seat where her boyfriend was once sitting.

"Mom, is this the guy you love?" I remarked without hesitation. "Because to me, he just isn't it."

"Rylie, what have I told you about giving him a chance? I know you don't like him, but he means no harm. He's really friendly, as you can see," Mom countered sternly. "You don't have to like him. All I'm asking for is for you to respect him and give him a chance. I know all these changes are difficult for you, but please, just try. Don't give him a hard time."

Her words stuck to me. It hit me that every time I was with Kaden, he was friendly and I was cold. He showed who he was, yet I didn't give him any chances. The words 'you don't have to like him' haunted me. Sure, I didn't like him at all -- I still don't, but I should still respect him. At least until he gives me a reason to not respect him as a person, which he hasn't done yet.

Maybe Mom is right. Maybe I should give him a chance. Hopefully, this Kaden guy won't prove Mom wrong in any sort of way.

We'll see.

***

"Boo!" A voice from behind me shouted as I practically jumped, holding on to dear life by grasping onto the rim of a counter. I was in Taco Fiesta, hoping to get my hands on some delicious tacos (and to see Elias if he was on a shift). Turns out, I will get to do and see both.

Elias was behind me, his big Tom Holland-like smile spread across his face. Instead of being in his hoodie and jeans from earlier during the school day, he was in his work uniform, a polo black shirt with Taco Fiesta's logo and black jeans, alongside a black baseball cap to top it off.

"Elias, you scared the shit out of me," I exclaimed as I cupped my hand over my chest.

"Sorry, Princess," Elias apologized with a chuckle as he went behind the counter, typing a few things into the register. I couldn't help but laugh at the cliché nickname. It definitely didn't suit me. Not one bit, which is what made it funny.

"It's okay, Green Bean," I played along. This nickname made more sense, considering that his last name is Greene, so it matched him perfectly.

"Good to hear. Now, what can I get you?" He mooned into my eyes.

"I'll take two classic tacos, alongside a small Fanta," I recited as I watched him type everything into the register.

"Perfect. That'll be eight fifty-five, but I'll put everything on me," Elias nodded. "Don't worry."

"Elias," I nagged, digging into my back pocket to search for money. "You don't have to do that for me."

"I know I don't have to, but I want to. It'll be my treat to you," he said as his hands over-lapped. I bet it was a tactic to try to convince me. I couldn't really say no.

"Fine," I huffed in a sarcastic manner, trying to match the tone of a young child compromising to something they didn't want to do.

Elias nodded as he went back to the kitchen area to grab my order. Moments later, he came back with a brown, paper bag. He placed a wrapped straw and napkins into the bag before grabbing a cup. He placed ice into it before placing the drinking fountain on Fanta, the nozzle letting out the carbonated drink. The fountain let out a huge puff.

"Here you go, Rylie," he said with a smile before he handed the contents to me. "I'll go sit with you. My break starts soon, anyway."

"That's great," I nodded as my face lit up. We walked to an idle booth and sat across from each other. I took both of the individually wrapped tacos out of the paper bag, pushing one towards him. "Want one?"

"Nah, I'm not hungry. Thanks, though," Elias said as he gently pushed it back to me. I shrugged before unwrapping one of the tacos, the zesty smell prickling my nose. My eyes focused on Elias as I took a bite out of the taco, who was looking at me back at every move I made.

"Stop looking at me," I teased as I dabbed the corner of my mouth with my napkin.

"Sheesh, aggressive much," he mocked in a playful manner, a laugh escaping his lips. "It's just so hard not to look at you. You're so appealing to look at."

"Okay, you win this time," I gave in with an sarcastic eye roll before biting into my taco.

"Figured," Elias curtly nodded as he adjusted his posture to slightly get closer to me. "I'm glad you decided to stop by here. Otherwise, work would've been so lonely and boring."

"I wanted to stop by. I was pretty bored at home, anyway," I remarked. It was true. All I had left to do there was homework. Was it a good idea to skip that and come here? Of course not, but homework can wait. I was hungry, anyway.

"So how is everything going at home? You know, with your mom and that guy you said she was dating? Well, that's if you mind sharing," Elias questioned as he took off his baseball cap, placing it onto the far end of the table.

"Eh . . . things are okay, I guess. He came over today, and I still don't like him," I admitted as I poked my straw into my drink. "My mom says I don't have to like him, but she wants me to respect him, and I'm trying to work my way up to that. I'm just still in disbelief about everything."

"And you don't have to like him just yet. But obviously, you should give him a chance. Is he nice?"

"I mean, my mom says he is. He does act friendly, but what if it's all an act?" I doubted. "I barely know this guy, yet my mom says that she's been dating him for about a year."

"If they've gotten that far into their relationship, that could mean that he's been good to your mom this entire time. He seems nice," Elias suggested with a shrug.

"You have a point. I guess I didn't think about that," I grimaced.

"I don't blame you. Just don't stress about it too much," he remarked as extended his hand. I dusted any possible crumbs off my hands and met his. He is such a great listener, which is one of the many things I love about him. He's also extremely supportive, and I adore that very much. I can't help but say that I'm extremely glad to have him as my boyfriend. It may have only been a few weeks since I first started dating him, but it felt like a lifetime.

Every moment with him felt so magical. I couldn't ask for anything more. Who knew that being in love could feel so . . . good?

30. Coming Out

ELIAS

HAVE YOU EVER felt like a third wheel to any sort of conversation before? You know, the feeling where you felt left out and irrelevant to anything and everything? That's how I feel right now, but in this case, I don't mind.

Cannon, Axel, and I were walking to our last class of the day — art. Cannon and Axel were deep in conversation about their families. They insist that they have grown to be sort of close over the years, considering they live in the same area. You know, ridiculously huge mansions with tons of land surrounding them.

I couldn't help but notice that the two have become closer than ever over the past few weeks. I don't want to be the one to assume, but was it possible that they were becoming attracted to each other romantically? It could be possible, but there was only one way to find out.

Once we got into class, Axel and Cannon separated so Axel could go chat with a friend for a bit, and Cannon and I sauntered to our usual table. Class hadn't started yet, so I said, "Are you and Axel? You know . . ." I questioned as I began to make hand signals.

"No, no, it's not like that, Eli," Cannon shook his head as he slouched down onto the table. "I don't even think he's my type and all, but he's still cool."

"Well, okay. I was just curious," I shrugged. "I know that he did say something about his parents being super conservative. Has he . . . come out to his parents yet?"

I know I was being very nosy, but at the end of the day, I just wanted to know. "He hasn't, but I'm trying to convince him to whenever he feels ready," he answered.

My eyes lit up, feeling a sensation of hope. I didn't know Axel's parents at all, but I'm hoping that everything goes fine when he comes out to them.

But concerning Axel and Cannon, no matter if they were just friends or something a little more, I will support them no matter what. If Cannon could finally find someone that he loves just as much as they love him, it would put a smile on my face. I've known for a long time that he's always wanted to find love. A lot of us do at some point. It's an amazing feeling, a feeling that isn't like any other.

Speaking of love, I saw Rylie walk into class, an opened book in hand as she glanced at it occasionally. She trudged to our usual table, clutching her fingers on the back of my neck playfully before taking a seat beside me.

"Hey," she chirped as she shoved her book into her backpack. I couldn't help but notice the blue cover of the book, alongside two black and white clouds at the center of it.

"Hi," I smiled. "What book are you reading?"

"The Fault in Our Stars by John Green," she replied briefly. "It's probably my millionth time reading it, but it's really good."

"Oh, cool," I chirped. Reading wasn't too much of my thing, but that's when a grand idea popped up in my head. "Hey, how about if we meet up at the local Barnes and Noble after school? We can grab a cup of coffee from their Starbucks and hang out for as much there."

"Sounds like a plan, Greene," Rylie nodded her head with approval. "I have to remember to bring some money. There's been books I've been dying to purchase."

"Glad to hear it, Henderson," I remarked before Ms. Edwards cleared her throat to get everyone's attention. This is my last class of the day, so I was looking forward to any art assignment thrown at me. Ms. Edwards explained that we would be making a series of complex patterns on a blank sheet of paper. It's a simple assignment, but she strictly instructed for us to not create everyday patterns, such as checkerboard squares, stripes, or polka dots.

Our patterns would have to be drawn out first, then colored with chalk. Yes, chalk. Not the kind that young children would use for hopscotch boards, but general chalk. The assignment will be due by the end of this week, so I would have to hustle to get this done. I ripped out a sheet of paper from my sketchbook specifically for this class, wrote my name on the bottom corner, then started to brainstorm ideas.

"What are you going to do?" Rylie questioned as she glanced at my blank paper.

"Hmm..." I hummed. That's when an idea hit me. "I think I'm going to do a bunch of shapes and color them sunset colors with a cool golden yellow outline around each shape. I hope it turns out well."

"That sounds so much better than what I'm going to do, for sure," Rylie stated without hesitation. "I'm going to do a weird circle pattern. You know, one that loops over and over again."

"That's still cool, Rylie. I'm sure it'll turn out great," I reassured her, cupping my hand over hers on the table slightly.

"You're just saying that because I'm your girlfriend," she teased with a chuckle.

"It's more than just that. I think that it has great potential," I nodded my head.

"Aww, look at the two lovebirds," Cannon recited in a mushy, high-pitched voice.

"So adorable," Axel added as he clasped his hands together.

"Shut up, you two," I remarked playfully with a laugh. I wanted to reach across the table to nudge their shoulders, but that would be too much work. Plus, I have work to do. It was Tuesday, meaning that we'd have the rest of class today, Wednesday, Thursday, and the beginning of Friday to finish up.

This assignment is an assignment that I'm looking forward too. I won't have to do any tedious research through textbooks or any math formulas to observe. All the assignment calls for is creativity, which weirdly interests me. That's just what art is.

***

About an hour after school, Rylie and I were walking through the tall doors of Barnes and Noble. The thick, awakening aroma of coffee hit my nose the moment we got into the establishment. We sauntered towards the built-in Starbucks. I ordered a Frappuccino, while Rylie ordered a cup of coffee. Once we paid and received our orders, I let Rylie led the way to the Young Adult section, where she carefully caressed every book, she touched as if she were holding on to a newborn baby's hands.

"You must really like books," I mentioned before taking a sip of my Frappuccino, the sweet caramel taste watering my mouth.

"I really do. Reading is like . . . my getaway from everything else, you know?" she sighed dreamily as she skimmed the back cover of a novel.

"I know how that feels. I feel the exact same way with art. It's one thing I could spend forever and ever doing," I said as I leaned on a bookshelf slightly.

"Yes! You actually get it!" Rylie cheered as she hugged a book to her chest. "I'm getting this. I hear that it's okay."

I skimmed the cover. The book was called The Girl Who Fell from the Sky. I don't think I've ever heard of this novel, but it seems interesting, judging the title.

"Do you want to sit down at the Starbucks to start reading it a little bit?" I offered as I pointed to the built-in Starbucks, not too far away from where we were.

"I'll sit down, but I think I'll start reading when I get home. When I start reading a book, I usually can't let go of it," Rylie chuckled as she motioned me to the coffee shop. We took a seat at a round table near the back of the Starbucks. At that moment, something hit me.

"You know, you've come a long way. You've definitely opened up, at least from when I first met you, Rylie," I proposed.

"I guess I can say that I've grown really comfortable with you, Elias. I feel like I could talk to you about anything and everything," Rylie mustered a smile before taking a sip of her coffee, pushing her book to the rim of the table so coffee wouldn't somehow accidentally spill over it.

"I'm glad that you feel that way. If there's anything you want to talk about ever, I'm here for you," I offered as I glimpsed at her luscious, red-ish brown-ish lips. I have to say this, she's really good at kissing, but I'm going a little of the rails right now. This is more of a serious conversation.

"Thanks for letting me know," she acknowledged. Without hesitation or doubt, I leaned in, her lush lips connecting to mine. I brushed her cheek with my hand before letting go of the kiss, remembering that we were in public. As much as I wanted to continue, I didn't want to create too much of a scene, considering that a middle-aged barista was staring at us from the counter. It was an uncomfortable feeling that honestly made me itch on the inside.

So instead, I brought up a topic. You know, to flirt and stuff.

"Honestly, back when school first started, I didn't think that things would turn out like this," I reflected as I felt my fingers grasping onto to my Frappuccino's plastic cup. "You know, getting to date such a cute girl — you — and just, getting to know you. It's a nice experience."

She giggled. "Oh my God, why does everything you say have to be so mushy and adorable, Elias? Care to explain?"

She was definitely flirting back.

"I just love you a lot, Rylie. I don't know how else to say it," I remarked.

"And I love you too," she replied as she motioned me to put my hands flat on the table. I did as instructed before she blanketed her hands on top of mine. Her hands felt like clouds. I didn't know for sure what clouds felt like, but I imagine them being the softest things ever. I know that they don't feel like anything, scientifically speaking, but getting back to the topic, her hands were warm, compared to my slightly rough hands. Rylie's hands were perfect to just hold out of comfort. That's how soft her hands actually were.

The vibration of my phone through my back pocket sounded, loud enough for us both to hear. I hesitated to see what the notification was, but instead, I let the phone vibrate and continued to stare at her. I stared at her nicely arched eyebrows, her tight curls, and her caramel skin, a few blemishes here and there. Nothing too visible. Honestly, she is still beautiful, regardless of anything considered an "imperfection."

To my surprise, my phone continued to buzz like crazy, making the annoying default Apple notification noise. Rylie nudged to me that it was okay to check it, so I did. The first thing that popped up on my notifications were recent text messages from Cannon.

Cannon, 3:49 PM: OMG!!

Axel just texted me and said that he was going to come out to his parents over dinner sometime this week. He finally said that he was ready!!

I texted back within an instant. This was huge news.

Me, 3:50 PM: That's great. Tell me how it goes tomorrow at school.

"You seem happy. What happened?" Rylie asked out of curiosity.

"Cannon just told me that Axel is going to come out to his parents," I explained briefly. "I'm actually excited for him."

"That's great. Hopefully it all turns out well," Rylie assured.

"Hopefully," I echoed.

At the beginning of the school year — or ever, really — Axel and I weren't on the best of terms. We were practically enemies, but now, I'm not really sure what we are. We've come to understand more and more about each other. Sure, we can be a little competitive with each other, but now, it's not that big of a deal. Either way, I'm just hoping that everything goes okay when he comes out to his parents.

I'll find out soon.

31. Arrangements

RYLIE

THE CLASSROOM WAS emptying more and more every minute as I struggled to place all my supplies into my backpack. It was a Friday afternoon after school, and like any normal person, I was hurrying to turn in my work so I could meet my friends at Taco Fiesta after school. It would be me, Elias, Nora, Cannon and Axel. This was scheduled to find out what his parent's response to him coming out and to support him.

I trudged to Ms. Edwards' desk and handed her our assignment. The objective was to create a complex pattern using all creativity possible. I think I did a pretty decent job with mine. I created this weird circular design on my paper using multiple colors all blending into one eventually. It sounds complicated, but it's really simple. I expect to at least get a B on my work because in my opinion, what I did was sort of common.

"Hey, come on. We don't want the others leaving us, do we?" Elias questioned with a chuckle.

"Yeah, I think Cannon and Axel are already outside in the parking lot. I saw them head out," Nora informed before plopping her sleek, raven hair to her shoulders.

"Oh, then we should hurry. I don't have my own car to drive to Taco Fiesta, and you don't either Elias . . ." I muttered as I gestured them around a corner that would eventually lead us to the student parking lot. "Also, do you even have your car, Nora?"

"It's broken. I couldn't even get it to start this morning," Nora groaned with an eyeroll. "So, when I get home, I have to convince my parents to let me take it the shop to get it fixed as soon as possible."

I wasn't really surprised. Out of everyone else, I would know that Nora's car is known for being all loud and raggedy. I remember on the end of the first day of school or something like that, the engine was so loud to the point where I thought that the car would break down right then and there. Actually, scratch that. Every time I'm in Nora's car is when I feel like it's going to break down. That's just how bad the performance of her car is.

So, I assured her. "I'm sure it's just a problem with your engine."

"Yeah, but just imagine what it would be like to have a fresh new ride like Cannon or Axel. I mean look at their cars," Nora joked as she pointed to their cars. At this point, we were already outside. "Could never be me."

Both of the boys had fancy, luxurious cars that I probably could never afford, so Nora did have a point. Speaking of the boys, once they saw us coming, they dove into their cars and started them up. Elias and I decided to ride with Cannon, while Nora wanted to ride with Axel.

"I call dibs on the front seat," Elias remarked as he grabbed the handle before I could even touch it.

"Shit," I rolled my eyes with a smile. "I'm too late."

"Unfortunately," he smiled, then paused. "But seriously, if you want front seat, it's all yours, Rylie."

"No, I'll be fine in the back. I'll have it all to myself, anyway," I chirped as I nudged his shoulder playfully.

"I insist, madam," Elias remarked with a fake French accent which honestly sounded horrible. But he tried, at least.

"You two argue but flirt at the same time like an old married couple. It's cute, though," Cannon joked as he honked his horn. "Get in the car already before I leave you both."

"Alright, slow your roll. We have all afternoon, sheesh," Elias chuckled as he placed his backpack on the floor, fastening his seatbelt after.

Cannon added. "Yeah, we do have all afternoon, but aren't you dying to know how his parents responded to him coming out? He did it last night."

"Point taken," I nodded as I watched him pull out of our parking space on the web cam screen.

It's a moment that we've all been waiting for, really. Deep down, all of us wanted to know what happened. The moment couldn't have come soon enough when we were settled at Taco Fiesta. The restaurant was busy, but not too busy. Mr. Mercado generously treated us all to a free meal each, all on the house.

"So," Axel sighed heavily as his eyes closed shut. "I told my parents that I'm bi." He paused for a bit and looked down at his Sprite. The carbonated drink was in a clear cup, so I watched the miniature bubbles inside the drink fizz up and connect to each other. The mood of the table we were all sitting at was tense, awaiting for an answer.

Cannon placed an arm on his shoulder with assurance. "You know, if you're not ready to tell us now, you don't have to."

"No, I just need to say it right now and get it over with," Axel insisted. "They didn't really understand at first, which I expected. They still want to stick with their conservative ways, however, they said that they respect my decision and such, but you know, they still don't really the support the fact that I'm bi and stuff."

"Sorry to hear that . . ." Elias said solemnly.

"It's all good. I'll get through it all," Axel combed his shaggy, raven hair with his fingers.

"Look, if you ever want to talk about it, we'll be here," Cannon assured as he patted his back. "We support you." In sync to this, the rest of us nodded in agreement.

"That's good to know," Axel muttered before taking a sip out of his Sprite.

After that, it was plain silence, besides the low background trumpet music playing and spatulas and spoon crashing against grills in the kitchen. The door of the establishment swung open as a girl with loose, caramel curls staggered in. It wasn't just any girl. It was Adrienne. None of us expected her to come here today, I know I didn't.

"Oh, it's a surprise to see you all here," Adrienne mustered a smile. To my surprise, Axel actually smiled back just a little. He doesn't smile normally, from what I know.

"Wanna sit with us?" He offered politely. "We can make room."

"Sure, but not for long, though," the girl glanced at her smart watch. "I have to visit my grandmother in half an hour."

She took a seat next to me, since I was on the end on my side of the booth we were situated at. She smelled sweet, like perfume. Now that I think about it, I haven't talked to her since I found her in the bathroom crying. You know, the day where her and Axel broke up. I didn't want to directly ask her about it since her ex-boyfriend was literally right there. So instead, I simply questioned, "How has everything been?"

"Everything's been okay, lately. It could be better, but I'm doing alright. Thanks for asking," Adrienne mustered a smile, then turned to everyone else. "What are you all doing here?"

"I had to tell them something pretty important," Axel said, looking up at the girl, but glancing back down at the table.

"Oh . . ." Adrienne nodded before her eyes lit up. "Oh!"

Adrienne looked as if she knew exactly what he was talking about. She probably did, or at least had an idea of what he was talking about, but I'd never know. The possibilities were endless.

***

When I got home, I was welcomed in by my cat, Cookie. She kept on trying to play with my shoelaces, even after I took my shoes off. I picked her up from the floor and carried her to the living room, where Mom and her boyfriend were watching a reality show on our flatscreen TV. Well, Mom was the only one who looked invested in it, judging the comments she was making to the ladies on there as if she were actually on the show. Kaden, however, was just nodding at every single thing she said, trying his best to fit in.

"Hey, Rylie," Kaden was quick to say with a wave. "How was your day at school?"

"My day was okay," I muttered as I slouched down on an armchair, carefully caressing the area behind Cookie's ears. In response, she purred. That meant that she liked it, so I continued to do it out of habit.

"That's good," Mom said before looking back at the TV. "Oh, come on, why did she have to do that?"

I raised an eyebrow as I stared at the television. I had absolutely no context of what was even going on in that show she was watching. All I saw were a bunch of ladies arguing with each other like children, but at the same time, like seniors. It was nothing but confusing.

Kaden turned to me. "What's your cat's name? She seems nice."

"Her name is Cookie," I answered briefly, slightly getting up to pass her to him. "Wanna hold her?"

"Sure," the man nodded as he gently grabbed her. "When I was about your age, I remember having a cat. It was so nice."

"Yeah, getting Cookie was cool," I nodded in agreement. "I actually got her over a year ago. No regrets."

"That's exactly how I felt when I got my cat," Kaden agreed. He tried to hand Cookie back to me, but instead of her acting like her normal, friendly self, she hissed. Kaden set the cat back down on his lap, causing her to purr. I knew Cookie well. Based on the way she was acting, she probably liked Mom's boyfriend very much.

It wasn't that big of a surprise because Cookie is a sweetheart, but if my own cat is already used to Kaden, how am I not used to him just yet?

Maybe I let my ego get in the way of respecting Kaden way too much, all because I missed Dad. Mom's words kept ringing in my head. She said I didn't have to like him, but I at least had to give him a chance. He seemed like a sweet guy with no bad intentions, but all this time of knowing him, I wasn't so nice to him.

And that's where I went wrong.

At that moment, my mom excused herself to go to the restroom. Besides the repetitive bickering of the women on Mom's reality show, the room was oddly silent. Since no one else was around, I could use this moment as an opportunity to at least apologize to Kaden for how I've treated him. I may have not said anything too smart to him since knowing him, but I did make things unnecessarily tense at times before today, like the time we were having dinner at his place. I automatically jumped into conclusions, which I now realize that I shouldn't have done.

"Kaden, I have something to tell you," my voice trailed off as I stared at Cookie, who was still situated on his lap, cozy and snug. "I'm sorry for how I've been acting around you lately."

I then began to explain how I felt about everything, like how I once believed that Kaden was there to replace my actual dad. I've come to realize that Mom needed someone after being alone for so long. Kaden, of course, understood everything.

"It's all good, Rylie. I love your mom very much and I do wish to spend the rest of my life with her, but don't feel pressured to call me "dad" ever. You don't have to," Kaden reasoned soothingly. "I don't mind at all because I'm not here to replace anyone. Whatever you want to call me is fine by me."

I nodded in agreement. Everything happened on such short notice, so I didn't feel like I was in the position to call him "dad" just yet, but I was glad that he was so understanding about everything. It's not every day where you find someone like that.

Kaden rummaged something out of his pocket. It looked like a small box, which probably had some kind of locket or necklace inside. He opened the box, directing it towards me. My eyes widened in shock of what was inside. It was a beautiful ring, which could only mean one thing. "I plan on proposing to your mother with this ring," Kaden sort of whispered, so Mom wouldn't hear from a distance away in case she was lurking around. "Do you like it?"

"Do I like it?" I echoed with awe. "I love it." I actually meant it.

"That's great, but how do you feel about me proposing to your mom so soon? I know that you just found out about her and I dating just a while ago . . ." the man questioned as he put away the ring.

"It all still feels unreal, but my mom really loves you and has been extremely happy lately, so I'm okay with it," I said with a smile. It was a real smile. Probably any day before today, I wouldn't have the courage to say that. My ego wouldn't have allowed me to, but now that I've thought about it, my mom really loved this guy. Whenever she'd used to lecture me about giving him a chance, she'd always sound so mushy and gushy talking about him. She was happy for the first time in forever, and that's all that mattered to me.

"Glad to hear it. I'm going to propose tomorrow evening at a new restaurant here in town. I made reservations, so we'll be all set," Kaden informed, keeping his voice low. I could see the hearts all up in his eyes. He really loved this woman. "Just don't tell her about it at all. I want it to be a surprise."

I nodded as I spotted Mom appear from around the corner. She took a seat where she was originally sitting on the couch next to her soon-to-be fiancé.

"I was just telling Rylie about dinner tomorrow. I made reservations at a restaurant tomorrow, so I'll come pick you two up, love," Kaden informed my mom, whose eyes lit up.

"Oh, really? I'll be looking forward to that," Mom cooed as she held onto his arm. "Thank you so much, babe."

"It's all on me," Kaden responded as he forked a hand through her hair gently.

I can't believe I'm saying this, but I'm looking forward to the proposal. This should be exciting to see.

32. Their Story

RYLIE

THE AROMA OF my strawberry cheesecake prickled my nose as I took a good last bite out of it. It was pretty decent for a cheesecake, if I say so myself. It was a nice Saturday, around eight-ten in the evening the last time I checked, which just so happened to be when we got here. I would take out my phone and check again, but Mom had a strict rule that phones couldn't be out during dinner. That typically applied when we were at home, so I didn't know if I could try to sneak my phone out here at the restaurant.

I wasn't going to try it this time, however. Mom seemed to be in a nice mood, and I didn't want to ruin it. She was in a salmon pink floral dress with matching hoop earrings. Her hair was straightened and wrapped into a high bun, topping the entire outfit off. It was dinner, so of course she would dress nice, but she didn't exactly know what she was getting into. Kaden hadn't yet proposed to her just yet, but I could tell he was nervous. At times, I saw him try to reach into his pocket to retrieve the ring case, but he resisted. He was probably trying to wait for the perfect time to do it.

Dinner was great. In fact, it was at the same restaurant Elias, and I ate out at the day he won second place for his art contest. The same friendly waitress who served us on that day also served us today. When she first saw me, she winked, but didn't say anything. Mom didn't know that we ate out here, and I made plans to keep it that way. At least for tonight because it was her night.

When the waitress rounded back to our table, Kaden fully paid for our entire meal, and we all prepared to head out. That was until he got up and stood before Mom, who was sitting down. Kaden knelt down before her on one knee, finally pulling out the ring case. He opened it, revealing the elegant ring inside.

"Madeline Archer, I am extremely lucky to have you in my life. I knew that you were the one the moment we first laid eyes. I am deeply in love with you, and I want nothing but the best for you and your daughter," he proclaimed, snatching the attention from other nearby families and couples situated at other tables. "Will you make me the happiest man alive and marry me?"

Mom's eyes widened in shock as her mouth dropped to her jaw. Tears began to stream down her face. "Yes, Kaden, yes!"

She leaned down to kiss him on his lips before holding out her hand so he could put the ring on her finger. People nearby clapped for them, congratulating them and all. After giving my mom a warm, snug hug for what seemed like forever, Kaden approached me as I stood up and gave me a hug that lasted just as long. Everyone genuinely looked happy. My mom was happy, Kaden was happy, so I was happy as well. I've never seen my mom cry tears of joy so much, but it made me feel all tingly inside. Kaden himself looked like he was about to tear up, as well.

It was an emotional moment for us all. Even the people in our surroundings took it to heart by congratulating as we walked past them. Once we were out of the restaurant, we situated ourselves in Kaden's BMW. For the entire ride home, the two flirted with each other back and forth. They couldn't get enough of themselves. It was sort of made me cringe to watch my mother act so flirtatious with her fiancé, considering that I was right there, watching and listening to them the entire time, but whatever made their boat float, I guess.

When we arrived home, around fifteen minutes or so later, instead of just dropping us off and driving to his apartment complex, Kaden escorted us inside. Since they weren't glued to the seats of the car anymore, their flirting just got worse. Now, they were being extremely touchy with each other.

"Get a room," I insisted with a grimace before climbing up the flight of stairs to get to my bedroom. Once I got there, I closed the door shut behind me and rummaged my phone out of my purse, texting Elias instantly afterwards. It turns out that he already texted me a sweet goodnight message because he knew that I'd be out to dinner and didn't know how long I'd stay out.

I texted him back with satisfaction, holding my phone up to my heart. All day before dinner, we've been texting and calling each other back and forth like we normally would on any other weekend. It always gave me a stable feeling just to talk with him. It was like he was my source of happiness in a way. I guess that's how my mom feels about Kaden, especially since she got proposed to just now.

She was truly happy, and I was, as well.

***

The following Monday during lunch period, Elias and I were situated at a table, rambling about anything and everything we could possibly think of. I was informing him about the proposal that happened recently on Saturday as he listened carefully.

"That's great, Rylie. I see you've finally gotten used to your mom's now fiancé?" Elias questioned. The last time I mentioned Kaden to him was when I was complaining to him of how I didn't like him and such, but things have drastically changed.

"Yeah, he's a pretty cool guy, to be honest," I admitted before spooning strawberry yogurt into my mouth. "He makes my mom so happy. Like, she's been in such a nice mood lately."

"That's nice to hear. I'm glad that everything worked out for you and your mom," he nodded before rummaging a notebook out of his backpack. He flipped to a page with a girl drawn in the middle and pushed the book towards me. The girl wasn't colored yet, but she had the same curly hair as me and an outfit I'd definitely wear — a hoodie and leggings.

"This is you. I've been working on this since this morning in between classes and such, but my sketch isn't finished, though. I have to add few minor details," Elias insisted as he looked down at his sketch, then back up at me. "What do you think about it?"

"It's so beautiful, I love it, Greene bean," I raved as I pushed his sketchbook back to him.

"You and that nickname," he smirked. "But seriously, I was thinking of painting a picture of you and hanging it up in my bedroom, alongside the previous ones I made with Cannon and my parents on them."

That's when my memory went back to the time where I first went in his bedroom. He did have paintings of his best friend, his parents, and himself on them. They were all people extremely close to him, so I found it sweet as hell when he said that his next painting would be of me. He loved me that much to the point where he was willing to paint a whole portrait of me. Now that take commitment.

"You'd actually do that for me?" I said, my voice sort of high pitched.

"Anything for you," he hummed before putting his sketch book away.

At that moment, the first bell rang, signalizing that our lunch period was over. Elias and I disposed of our trash before meeting Nora and Cannon at the entrance of the lunchroom.

"We saw you two eat lunch together. Ugh, you two are the cutest, I swear," Nora remarked as she grabbed my arm.

"Yeah, little Elias is growing up," Cannon added teasingly before nudging his shoulder.

"You remind me of my dad. Always embarrassing me," Elias joked before planting his arm behind his neck. "Cannon, we have to get to History now since it's on the west wing of the building." He turned to me and planted a quick kiss on my cheek, then said, "I'll see you later, Henderson. I love you."

"Love you, too," I said as I watched the two turn round a corner.

"He's literally the sweetest boyfriend ever," Nora remarked as we climbed up a flight of stairs. "You know, you've definitely come a long way. I remember the times where you wouldn't even talk to anyone, but now, look at you. You got a whole boyfriend. I'm so proud of you."

I nodded at her response, letting it all sink it. I do remember the times at the beginning of this school year where I just wanted to disappear whenever I was in the presence of people. It's hard to think that that was me several months ago. But now, it's safe to say that I've opened up a bit. I don't regret it one bit. Since I've branched out, I've felt like a better person.

I know that's what Mom wanted. I know it's what Nora wanted, Cannon and Elias, as well. Even Dad would want that for me if he were still alive. It's just amazing how I managed to turn everything around just like that. In a good way, too. If I got the opportunity to look into a crystal ball to see the future earlier this school year, I wouldn't have believed that this would be how I turned out.

But life can surprise you in so many ways, good and bad. But this was an example of life surprising me in a good way.

***

A few hours later after school, Elias and I found ourselves at my doorstep. I insisted on him coming over so we could hang out. Plus, he's never been to my place, so I wanted to show him around.

"Do you think your Mom will like me?" Elias questioned as I fumbled my house key into the key hole to unlock it.

"She will. You're a sweet guy," I insisted as I grasped onto the door handle to open it. "Plus, this isn't your first time meeting her. Remember that one time when her and I were at Taco Fiesta, and you were there working? She seemed to like you then, so I don't see why she wouldn't like you now."

"Oh, yeah. You have a point," Elias said with a curt nod before slipping off his shoes. He placed them beside the front door as I did the same.

That's when Mom walked into the foyer, cradling Cookie in her arms, her mouth dropped open. "Hey, Rylie. You didn't tell me that you are inviting any guests over. If so, I would've prepared something to eat," Mom said with surprise before mustering a smile to Elias. "I remember you. Aren't you the guy that works at Taco Fiesta in town? Your name is . . ."

"Elias. And yeah, that's me. It's nice to see you again, Ms. Archer," Elias nodded. I guess he remembered that my mom went by a different last name than me.

That's when it hit me. From what I remember, I hadn't really given Mom an update. I only remember her teasing me about him, but I didn't inform her that he was now my boyfriend. This is going to come off as a surprise to her, I just know it.

Or she probably already knew. In her mind, she could've been trying to think of why else I brought a boy home. The possibilities were endless.

"Oh, are you two dating now or . . . ?" She questioned. I knew it.

"Yeah, Mom, we are," I said, nodding in approval.

"You kids grow up so fast," she remarked as she released Cookie to the ground. "Can I get you two anything to eat?"

"I'm good, but thanks, anyway," Elias replied briefly.

Mom nodded as she motioned us to the living room, as if we were restricted to stay there only. I didn't really mind too much, but a little privacy would sound nice. Elias took a seat on the main sofa, his backpack against his feet. Before I got the chance to sit down beside him, Mom stopped me. "Your boyfriend is so polite," she whispered, loud enough for Elias himself to hear.

"Mom," I whined before I sat down beside Elias. I could feel my cheeks heat up like flames, especially after he began to giggle. I guess it was my turned to be teased by my mom, considering that there were a few times Elias had gotten embarrassed by his own parents.

"Alright, alright. I need to head to work for a few hours. There's food in the fridge in case you're hungry," Mom announced before picking up her purse from the kitchen counter. "Just, you know the rules, Rylie. No baby-making while you two are here all alone."

"Okay," I hollered as I watched her disappear around a corner to the garage door. I couldn't help but feel a little more embarrassed since I had no intentions of doing that, but she just wanted to remind me. "Bye, Mom."

"Goodbye, Ms. Archer," Elias added.

Soon enough, it was Elias, Cookie, and I left in the room. I spooned my cat into my arms, rocking her back and forth like a baby.

"Nice cat you've got there," Elias complimented. "Her name is . . ."

"Cookie," I finished his sentence with a smile. "She's a sweetheart."

"I can tell that she is," he nodded as I handed the cat to him so he could hold her. "But you're the sweetest one here."

"Ugh, come here already," I hummed before planting my lips over his. Without any hesitation, he kissed back aggressively, yet softly at the same time. His mouth went lower and lower to my neck, which felt better than I thought it would.

"Elias," I moaned faintly as he worked his magic. It was just irresistible, like I was floating in the air. Except, I didn't want to come down.

"I love it when you call my name, Rylie," he hummed as he let go of kissing me, looking me straight into the eye. "I love you. It's crazy to think that you were that one hot girl I saw in art class on the first day of school, but now, I'm lucky enough to have you as my girlfriend."

"You're the sweetest, Elias. I love you, too," I murmured as I forked my hand through his curls. It was my way of fighting the urge to kiss him all over again. "It's been quite a journey for me to get to this point, but I wouldn't change anything. All I need is you."

I found myself leaning down on his shoulder as he brushed my shoulders with his fingers. It wasn't perfect because nothing is truly perfect, but it was flattering. Nora's words kept on ringing inside my head. I did come a long way. It might've been rough, but I wouldn't change anything for the world. I was fortunate enough to have a boyfriend who trusted and depended on me the same way I did to him.

Our story was ours, not one found inside a book. It wasn't perfect, but it wasn't overly emotional either. It didn't need to be. Our story was ours, and I couldn't ask for anything more. Life really can be good to you as long as you make it that way.

And that was more than enough for me.

www.ingramcontent.com/pod-product-compliance
Lightning Source LLC
Chambersburg PA
CBHW071216080526
44587CB00013BA/1395